Mastering Ruby

Ruby is a superb programming language used for a variety of activities such as developing desktop applications, static websites, computational services, and even automation systems. *Mastering Ruby: A Beginner's Guide* is a detailed guide for beginners to understand Ruby. This book discusses how to structure applications properly and organize code for optimum performance.

Concise and easy to understand, this book provides the fundamentals for web programming along with software development and simple app development. It covers a variety of topics, starting from syntax styles workflow for the Command line to creating websites that will quickly advance necessary information. This book explains how to structure applications properly and organize code for optimum performance.

The key principles about Ruby explained here are helpful to beginners and users interested in learning this highly technological and diverse language.

Key Features:

- Follows a hands-on approach and offers practical lessons and tutorials related to Ruby.

- Provides an in-depth discussion of Ruby design and applications to help build robust knowledge.

- Explains how to create individual websites using Ruby programming.

About the Series

The *Mastering Computer Science* covers a wide range of topics, spanning programming languages as well as modern-day technologies and frameworks. The series has a special focus on beginner-level content and is presented in an easy-to-understand manner, comprising:

- Crystal-clear text, spanning various topics sorted by relevance.

- Special focus on practical exercises, with numerous code samples and programs.

- A guided approach to programming, with step-by-step tutorials for the absolute beginners.

- Keen emphasis on real-world utility of skills, thereby cutting the redundant and seldom-used concepts and focusing instead of industry-prevalent coding paradigm.

- A wide range of references and resources, to help both beginner and intermediate-level developers gain the most out of the books.

The *Mastering Computer Science* series of books start from the core concepts, and then quickly move on to industry-standard coding practices, to help learners gain efficient and crucial skills in as little time as possible. The books assume no prior knowledge of coding, so even the absolute newbie coders can benefit from this series.

The *Mastering Computer Science* series is edited by Sufyan bin Uzayr, a writer and educator having over a decade of experience in the computing field.

For more information about this series, please visit: https://www.routledge.com/Mastering-Computer-Science/book-series/MCS

Mastering Ruby
A Beginner's Guide

Edited by
Sufyan bin Uzayr

CRC Press
Taylor & Francis Group
Boca Raton London New York

CRC Press is an imprint of the
Taylor & Francis Group, an **informa** business

First Edition published 2024
by CRC Press
2385 NW Executive Center Drive, Suite 320, Boca Raton, FL 33431

and by CRC Press
2 Park Square, Milton Park, Abingdon, Oxon, OX14 4RN

CRC Press is an imprint of Taylor & Francis Group, LLC

ISBN: 9781032415253 (hbk)
ISBN: 9781032415246 (pbk)
ISBN: 9781003358510 (ebk)

DOI: 10.1201/9781003358510

Typeset in Minion
by KnowledgeWorks Global Ltd.

For Mom

Contents

About the Editor

Sufyan bin Uzayr is a writer, coder, and entrepreneur having over a decade of experience in the industry. He has authored several books in the past, pertaining to a diverse range of topics, ranging from History to Computers/IT.

Sufyan is the Director of Parakozm, a multinational IT company specializing in EdTech solutions. He also runs Zeba Academy, an online learning and teaching vertical with a focus on STEM fields.

Sufyan specializes in a wide variety of technologies, such as JavaScript, Dart, WordPress, Drupal, Linux, and Python. He holds multiple degrees, including ones in Management, IT, Literature, and Political Science.

Sufyan is a digital nomad, dividing his time between four countries. He has lived and taught in universities and educational institutions around the globe. Sufyan takes a keen interest in technology, politics, literature, history, and sports, and in his spare time, he enjoys teaching coding and English to young students.

Learn more at sufyanism.com.

Acknowledgments

There are many people who deserve to be on this page, for this book would not have come into existence without their support. That said, some names deserve a special mention, and I am genuinely grateful to:

- My parents, for everything they have done for me.

- The Parakozm team, especially Divya Sachdeva, Jaskiran Kaur, and Simran Rao, for offering great amounts of help and assistance during the book-writing process.

- The CRC team, especially Sean Connelly and Danielle Zarfati, for ensuring that the book's content, layout, formatting, and everything else remain perfect throughout.

- Reviewers of this book, for going through the manuscript and providing their insight and feedback.

- Typesetters, cover designers, printers, and everyone else, for their part in the development of this book.

- All the folks associated with Zeba Academy, either directly or indirectly, for their help and support.

- The programming community in general, and the web development community in particular, for all their hard work and efforts.

—Sufyan bin Uzayr

Zeba Academy – Mastering Computer Science

The "Mastering Computer Science" series of books are authored by the Zeba Academy team members, led by Sufyan bin Uzayr, consisting of:

- Divya Sachdeva

- Jaskiran Kaur

- Simran Rao

- Aruqqa Khateib

- Suleymen Fez

- Ibbi Yasmin

- Alexander Izbassar

Zeba Academy is an EdTech venture that develops courses and content for learners primarily in STEM fields and offers educational consulting and mentorship to learners and educators worldwide.

Additionally, Zeba Academy is actively engaged in running IT Schools in the CIS countries and is currently working in partnership with numerous universities and institutions.

For more info, please visit https://zeba.academy.

## CHAPTER 1

Overview of Ruby

IN THIS CHAPTER

➢ Introduction

➢ Comparison of Java with Other Programming Languages

➢ Advantages

➢ Environment Setup in Ruby

➢ Installation of Ruby

➢ Facts about Ruby Programming Language

Ruby was developed by Yukihiro Matsumoto in Japan in the middle of the 1990s (commonly known as Matz in the Ruby community). Everything in Ruby is an object, with the exception of blocks; however, there are alternatives like procs and lambda. The purpose of Ruby was to provide a useful barrier between software developers and the underlying hardware. Because Ruby's syntax is similar to those of a number of programming languages, including C and Java, learning it is straightforward for developers proficient in those languages. All operating systems, including Windows, Mac, and Linux, are supported.[1]

Perl, Lisp, Smalltalk, Eiffel, and Ada are a few of the other languages that Ruby is based on. Since most implementations don't translate programs into assembly code before running instructions, it is an interpreted scripting language. The robust RubyGems may be used by Ruby developers as well (RubyGems provides a standard format for Ruby programs and libraries).

DOI: 10.1201/9781003358510-1

WHAT IS THE PURPOSE OF RUBY?

The general-purpose, flexible Ruby scripting language is used for a variety of activities.[2]

For developing desktop applications, static websites, computational services, and even automation systems, Ruby is a superb programming language. Web servers, DevOps, web scraping, and crawling, among other things, use it. And with the power of the Rails application framework, we can do much more, especially with database-driven web projects.

Ruby on Rails

As a high-level computer program, Ruby stands alone. However, it is hard to talk about Ruby without mentioning Rails.

The application framework Ruby on Rails (RoR) is responsible for propelling Ruby into the public eye, boosting its acceptance, and transforming it into a superb cloud language.

RoR, as defined by https://rubyonrails.org/, is "an open-source web framework intended for the programmer satisfaction and sustained performance."

For communication, file management, database connectivity, and other functions, the RoR framework includes prewritten Ruby code. It performs the time-consuming activities so we can focus on finding solutions. Don't Repeat Yourself, or DRY, is a core Rails principle that greatly enhances the effectiveness of the framework.

GitHub, Bloomberg, SoundCloud, Hulu, Twitch, Square, The Weather Channel, Basecamp, Airbnb, Hulu, Instacart, and Twitter are just a few of over a million websites built on RoR.

Ruby versus Python

One of the most popular comparisons for Ruby is with Python. It may be challenging for coders to choose which language to learn or use for a project because Ruby and Python share many similarities and can be used for many of the same objectives. Ruby and Python are both high-level server-side programming languages with straightforward syntax, yet they differ greatly technologically.

Some of the distinctions between Ruby and Python are as follows:

- Python supports several Integrated Development Environments (IDEs), but Ruby only supports EclipseIDE.

- Python is restricted to the Django framework, while Ruby is limited to Rails.

- Although Ruby has a robust blocks feature, Python has more libraries.

- Although Ruby is a simple object-oriented language, Python is more prevalent among data scientists. And so forth, tit for tat.

There are also more subtle distinctions.

- Ruby is harder to debug for certain programmers but more versatile, in general.

- Some people find Python simpler to comprehend at first but more suffocating in the long run.

WHAT IS THE POINT OF LEARNING RUBY?

The Ruby programming language is intended to increase developer productivity and enjoyment. Ruby is popular with programmers because it is high level and has a simple syntax. We have less code to write and can concentrate on solving our problems.

Because of Ruby's high-level and abstract nature, it is a simple language to learn and apply. While many low-level languages need hundreds of lines of code for the most basic of tasks, Ruby allows us to create our first cloud application in only a few hours.

According to the 2020 Stack Overflow Developer Survey, Ruby is the 14th most widely used programming language globally, with 7.1% of respondents working with RoR.

It's also a good alternative for swiftly developing applications and outperforms Python in web development.

START WITH RUBY SCRIPTING

Getting a Compiler

Before we begin writing in Ruby, we must first obtain a compiler to build and run our code. Several online compilers may use to get started with Ruby without having to install a compiler:

https://www.jdoodle.com/execute-ruby-online

https://repl.it/

There are several free compilers provided for Ruby software execution.

Ruby Programming

Because Ruby's grammar is similar to those of other commonly used languages, it is simple to learn.

Writing Ruby programs: Ruby programs may be developed in any of the frequently used text editors such as Notepad++, gedit, and so on. After we've finished writing the programs, save the file with the extension .rb.

Let's go through some fundamental programming concepts:

Comments: # (hash) is used to add single-line comments in Ruby programs.

Syntax:

```
# Comment
```

To make multiline comments in Ruby, use a block of =begin and =end (reserved Ruby keywords).

Syntax:

```
=begin
Statement1
Statement2
...
Statementn
=end
```

Example: A simple application prints "Hello Peeks, Thank you for visiting PeeksforPeeks."

```
# sample Ruby code
puts ' Hello Peeks, Thank you for visiting
PeeksforPeeks'
```

It is worth noting that the output screen shows how a code is configured to run on command.

Explanation: The first line is a single-line comment with the prefix "#." The second line contains the message to be printed, and puts is used to display the message on the screen.

Ruby, like everything else, has pros and cons.

BENEFITS OF RUBY

- Ruby code is compact, beautiful, and powerful because it contains fewer lines of code.

- Ruby provides quick and easy building of web applications, resulting in less effort.

- Because Ruby is free to copy, use, and edit, it enables developers to make modifications as and when they are needed.

- Ruby is a dynamic programming language; hence, there are no complex rules on how to implement features, and it is extremely near to spoken languages.

LIMITATIONS OF RUBY

- Ruby is very new and has its own unique coding language, making it challenging for programmers to code in it immediately, but it is simple to use with some experience. Many programmers prefer to stick to what they are already familiar with and capable of developing.

- Ruby code is more difficult to debug since it produces most of the time during runtime, making it tough to interpret when debugging.

- Compared to other programming languages, Ruby does not have an abundance of informative resources.

- Ruby is an interpreted scripting language, and because the programming language is often slower than compiled languages, Ruby is slower than many other languages.

APPLICATIONS

- Ruby is used to construct several types of web apps. It is currently a popular technique for developing web apps.

- Ruby has a fantastic functionality known as Ruby on Rails (RoR). It is a web framework developers use to speed up and save time throughout the development process.

JAVA VERSUS OTHER PROGRAMMING LANGUAGES COMPARISON

Java is a well-known and extensively used computer language and platform. A platform is an environment that facilitates the development and execution of programs written in any programming language.

Java is quick, dependable, and secure. Java is utilized everywhere, from desktop to online apps, scientific supercomputers to gaming consoles, cell phones to the Internet.

This section compares Java to three other languages (Python, C++, Ruby, and C).[3]

Python

- Python is a high-level programming language. Object-oriented programming is completely supported. Python is not strictly an object-oriented language.

- Java is a compiled computer program, whereas Python is an interpreted language.

- Java is a low-level implementation language, whereas Python is a scripting language.

- Python is simple to use; however, Java is more complicated. Programmers prefer Python over Java because it has less lines of code, whereas Java is the polar opposite.

- Python code is substantially shorter than Java code.

- Python is extensively used in businesses for project development since its programs are shorter; however, Java is seldom used in businesses for project development because it is harder to use.

- Python offers dynamic typing, which is particularly important for programmers since it requires them to write less code, which saves time and is user- and programmer friendly. However, in the case of Java, developers must declare the type of each variable before using it, which takes a long time.

- Python is used by many huge enterprises such as Google, Yahoo, NASA, and others. On the other hand, Python applications are typically anticipated to execute slower than Java programs.

- The primary benefit of Java is that it has considerably more excellent library support for various use cases than Python.

- Python is significantly slower than Java.

C++

- Java was derived primarily from C++.

- C++ is a procedural and object-oriented programming language, whereas Java is only object-oriented.

- Both languages have distinct goals, which imply they have significant differences.

- The primary goal of C++ is to create a programming system.

- Operator overloading is not supported in Java, but it is in C++.

- C++ expands the C programming language, whereas Java was designed primarily to allow network computing.

- Structures and unions are not supported in Java, although they are in C++.

- Java is significantly slower than C++ in terms of processing performance.

- C++ libraries are both simple and robust. Additionally, it supports container and associative arrays. However, Java has a robust cross-platform library.

- In Java, trash collection is automated; however, this is not the case in C++. All objects in C++ are destroyed manually with the aid of code.

- Pointers are variables in C++ that store the addresses of other variables. However, no variable in Java saves the addresses of other variables.

- C++ applications run much faster than Java ones.

Ruby

- Ruby and Java are both object-oriented and tightly typed languages.

- Ruby is dynamically typed, whereas Java is statically typed.

- Both languages have a unique way of executing code. Java translates the code first into computer language so it can be understood by it; as a result, Java code executes quicker than Ruby code.

- Both Java and Ruby provide inheritance and public, private, and protected methods.

- Because Ruby functions need less code lines than Java, it is selected first by programmers and designers.

C

- C is quite similar to C++ (which was used to derive Java). In reality, C++ is an improved version of C.

- C is a procedural or structure-oriented programming language, whereas Java is an object-oriented programming language.

- When compared to Java, C applications take much less time to execute.

- Java does not provide variables for storing addresses of other variables, although C does.

- C does not provide exception handling in its programs, but Java does.

DIFFERENCES AND SIMILARITIES BETWEEN RUBY AND C

C and Ruby have several similarities, including the following:[4]

- A coder can program procedurally if they want to. However, it will remain object-oriented behind the scenes.

- Both languages share operators such as compound assignment and bitwise operators. However, unlike C, Ruby does not have ++ or – with it.

- They both have __FILE__ and __LINE__ with them.

- Although there is no particular const keyword, we can still have constants.

- Strings are enclosed in double quotes in both C and Ruby, that is, "."

- They both contain changeable strings.

- Most documentation, including man pages, may be viewed using the ri command in our terminal.

- Both of them have the same type of command-line debugger.

Ruby	C
There is no need to build code in Ruby; it may run directly.	Because C code cannot run directly, it must be compiled.
It needs "foo" rather than #include or #include "foo."	Nothing of the sort is necessary in C.
Ruby does not have variable declarations.	In C, the variable declaration is required.
There are no macros or preprocessors in Ruby, as well as no casts, pointers, typedefs, sizeof, or enums.	They are, nevertheless, present in C.
Method arguments (i.e., functions) are supplied by value, with the values always being object references.	Functions in C can be passed by value or by reference.
Parentheses are not always required for method (or function) calls.	In C, this is not an option.
There is no char, only 1 letter strings.	In C, char refers to a single character.
In Ruby, array literals are enclosed in brackets rather than braces.	In C, array literals are enclosed in brackets.
We cannot select assembly.	We cannot select assembly in C.
Objects in Ruby are tightly typed.	Objects in C are not tightly typed.
If and while condition phrases are written without parentheses.	When using if and while expressions in C, parentheses are required.
Strings in Ruby do not finish with a null byte.	In C, while strings conclude with a null byte.
Instead of executing pointer arithmetic, when we combine two arrays, we receive a new and larger array (of course, created on the heap).	In C, pointer arithmetic is required.
Arrays in Ruby grow automatically as more elements are added to them.	In C, an array cannot grow automatically.
The heap contains all variables. Furthermore, you are not required to liberate them ourselves; the garbage collector will do it.	Because C lacks a waste collector, we must liberate them ourselves.
Braces are rarely used; multi-line structures (such as whileloops) are terminated with an end keyword.	Braces are essential since neglecting them will result in a syntactic error.
Because there are no header files in Ruby, all methods and classes are declared in the primary source code files.	In C, header files are present.
At the end of the lines, there aren't any semicolons.	There are some ending lines.
Ruby does not support #define. Simply use constants.	#define exists in C.
The do keyword is used for "blocks." There is no "do statement" like there is in C.	In C, the do statement is combined with the while statement to create a do-while loop.

DIFFERENCES AND SIMILARITIES BETWEEN RUBY AND C++

C++ and Ruby have numerous commonalities, some of which are as follows:[5]

- In Ruby, public, private, and protected work similarly to how they do in C++.

- In Ruby, inheritance syntax is still one character, but it's < instead of:.

- In the same manner that "namespace" is used in C++, we can place our code in "modules" in Ruby.

- There are numerous operators in Ruby that are comparable to those in C++.

- Although the keyword names have been modified to protect the innocent, exceptions function similarly.

Ruby	C++
Every variable in Ruby is simply an automatically dereferenced identifier for some object, which implies there are no explicit references in Ruby.	Unlike Ruby, C++ has explicit references.
Ruby objects are robust yet dynamically typed.	Objects in Python are not as highly typed as those in Ruby.
Instead of the class name, the "constructor" is named initialize.	In C++, this is not the case.
There are just two container types: array and hash.	In C++, there are several container types.
C++ templates are not required. No casting is also necessary.	C++ templates are required in this case. There is casting.
Instead of this, it's self.	Instead of self, it is this.
Iteration is carried out in a unique manner. There is no separate iterator object in Ruby. Instead, you utilize the container object's iterator function, which accepts a block of code and sends subsequent elements to it.	Vectors are necessary and utilized in C++, making writing more accessible.
Ruby includes lib, a unit-testing framework.	This is not possible in C++.
Ruby does not support type conversions.	In C++, type conversion is required.
There are some case conventions that must follow.	C++ does not have such case conventions, making it simple.
In Ruby, you may reopen a class at any moment and add extra methods.	This is not possible in C++.
In Ruby, certain methods terminate with a "?" or a "!" It is, in fact, part of the method name.	In C++, similar symbols are not necessary at the conclusion of methods.

(Continued)

Ruby	C++
In Ruby, all methods are always virtual.	In C++, methods are not virtual.
Multithreading is built in, although as of Ruby 1.8, it is referred to as "green threads" rather than "native threads."	Multithreading is not built into C++.
In Ruby, parentheses used to invoke methods are frequently optional.	Parentheses are essential in C++ and must be used.
There is no direct access to member variables; all access to public member variables is through methods.	In C++, member variables can access directly.

ENVIRONMENT SETUP IN RUBY

Ruby is a high-level, interpreted general-purpose scripting language. Ruby is a dynamically typed language that employs garbage collection. It accommodates a variety of programming paradigms, including object-oriented, procedural, and functional programming.[6] Ruby is built on the foundations of several other languages, including Perl, Lisp, Smalltalk, Eiffel, and Ada. This language has a beautiful syntax that is easy to read and write.

The Linux and Windows environmental parameters are mentioned below.

Steps for Installing the Ruby Environment on Windows

1. Ruby can be downloaded via https://rubyinstaller.org/downloads/
   Click on any link as our desired version based on our Windows, for instance, Ruby 2.6.4-1 (x64) for Windows(64 bit) and the second link which reads Ruby 2.6.4-1 (x86) for Windows(32 bit), which is the newest version, as noted here.

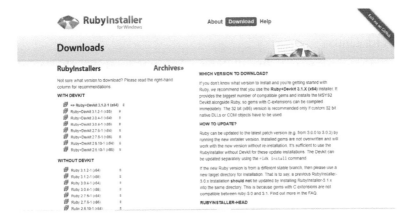

Download page of Ruby.

2. After downloading the software, double-click the .exe file and follow the on-screen instructions to install Ruby on our Windows computer. After installing Ruby with the default settings on Windows, we must configure the environment variable.

3. Navigate to System and Security -> System in the Control Panel. Then select Advanced System Settings and then select Environment Variables from the Advanced menu.

4. Now we must edit the "Path" variable under System Variables to include the path to the Ruby environment. Select the "Path" variable from the System Variables list and select the Edit button.

5. We'll get a selection of alternative paths; click the New button and then enter the path where Ruby is installed. Ruby is installed by default in the "C:\Ruby26-x64\bin" (in our instance) OR "C:\Ruby26-x86\bin" folder. If we installed Ruby in another location, add that to the path. For example, if we installed Ruby on another drive, go to that drive and locate the Ruby folder; inside the ruby folder, there will be a folder called bin; copy the path and include it in the System Variable's Path as SomeDrive:\SomeFolderRubyXX-xYY\bin.

6. We're done when we click OK and save the adjustments. Open the command prompt window and type "ruby –v" to see if the installation was successful. On the console, we should see something like ruby 2.6.4p104 (2019-08-28 revision 67798) [x64-mingw32] (in our case). It implies we've installed Ruby successfully and are ready to proceed.

Steps for Linux

There are various ways to install Ruby in Linux (Ubuntu), including utilizing third-party programs. However, we shall refer to the most basic and straightforward method of installing Ruby through terminal.

- Navigate to Application -> Terminal

- Type command, as seen below:

```
sudo apt install ruby-full
```

Then hit enter to insert our password. Wait for it to finish downloading before installing Ruby on our PC.

- We have completed the Ruby installation on Linux. In the Terminal, execute ruby -v to see if the installation was successful. If we see lines like ruby 2.6..., it signifies we've successfully installed Ruby on our Linux system.

Popular Ruby Editors/IDEs

- Notepad/gedit: These are simple text editors that can be used to write Ruby scripts. Notepad is a Windows program, whereas gedit is a Linux program.

- NetBeans: NetBeans is a well-known free IDE for building ruby-based software. NetBeans can be downloaded from this page.

HOW DO WE INSTALL RUBY ON LINUX?

Before we begin the installation of Ruby on Linux, we must first understand what Ruby is. Ruby is a pure object-oriented language created in Japan in the mid-1990s by Yukihiro Matsumoto (commonly known as Matz in Ruby community).[7] Except for blocks, everything in Ruby is an object; however, there are substitutes, such as procs and lambda. Ruby's creation aimed to provide a useful barrier between human developers and the underlying computing gear.

Ruby is built on the foundations of several other languages, including Perl, Lisp, Smalltalk, Eiffel, and Ada. It is an interpreted scripting language, meaning most implementations run instructions immediately and without first converting a program into machine-language instructions.

Installing and Downloading Ruby

Ruby for Linux can be downloaded and set up by typing the following command into the terminal (Ctrl + Alt + T):

```
$ sudo apt install ruby-full
```

To begin with, the installation

- Begin with command

- Accepting installation

- Obtaining files

- Files are being unpacked

- Organizing resources

- Installation is complete

To see if Ruby was installed correctly, use the following command on the terminal:

```
ruby --version
```

Here's an example program to get us started with Ruby programming: Consider a basic Hello Everyone program.

To begin, open a text editor such as Notepad or Notepad++ in the terminal. Create the code in a text editor and save it with the (.rb) extension.

To run the helloeveryone.rb Ruby script, type ruby helloeveryone.rb, and the result will be printed.

HOW DO WE INSTALL RUBY ON WINDOWS?

Before we begin the installation of Ruby on Windows, we must first understand what Ruby is. Ruby is a pure object-oriented language created in Japan in the mid-1990s by Yukihiro Matsumoto (commonly known as Matz in the Ruby community). Except for blocks, everything in Ruby is an object; however, there are substitutes, such as procs and lambda.[8] Ruby's creation aimed to provide a useful barrier between human programmers and the underlying computing gear.

Ruby is built on the foundations of several other languages, including Perl, Lisp, Smalltalk, Eiffel, and Ada. It is an interpreted scripting language, which means that most implementations run instructions immediately and without first converting a program into machine-language instructions.

Installing and Downloading Ruby

All versions of Ruby for Windows are available for download at https://rubyinstaller.org/downloads/. Download the newest version and follow the installation instructions.

To begin with, the installation

- Begin with a license agreement

- Choosing an installation location

- Choosing which components to install

- Extracting and installing files

- Installation is now complete

MYSYS2 Component Installation

- Select what to install

- Database updates and key signing

- Files are being installed

- Packages are being downloaded

- Package installation

To see if Ruby is successfully installed, use the following command on the command line:

```
ruby -v
```

Here's an example program to get us started with Ruby programming: Consider a basic Hello Everyone program.

```
puts "Hello Everyone"
```

Run the irb command from the command line. After that, we may write the Ruby code, which will execute through the command line.

This chapter covered the introduction, comparison of Java with other programming languages, and its advantages. Moreover, we covered environment setup in Ruby, installation of Ruby, and facts about Ruby programming language.

NOTES

1. Ruby programming language (introduction): https://www.geeksforgeeks. org/ruby-programming-language-introduction/, accessed on August 19, 2022.
2. What is the Ruby programming language?: https://acloudguru.com/blog/ engineering/what-is-the-ruby-programming-language, accessed on August 19, 2022.
3. Comparison of Java with other programming languages: https://www.geeks-forgeeks.org/comparison-of-java-with-other-programming-languages/
4. Similarities and differences between Ruby and C language: https://www. geeksforgeeks.org/similarities-and-differences-between-ruby-and-c-lan-guage/, accessed on August 19, 2022.

5. Similarities and differences between Ruby and C++: https://www.geeksfor-geeks.org/similarities-and-differences-between-ruby-and-c/, accessed on August 19, 2022.
6. Environment setup in Ruby: https://www.geeksforgeeks.org/environment-setup-in-ruby/, accessed on August 19, 2022.
7. How to install Ruby on Linux?: https://www.geeksforgeeks.org/how-to-install-ruby-on-linux/, accessed on August 19, 2022.
8. How to install Ruby on Windows?: https://www.geeksforgeeks.org/how-to-install-ruby-on-windows/, accessed on August 19, 2022.

## CHAPTER 2

OOP Concepts of Ruby

IN THIS CHAPTER

- ➢ Class and Object
- ➢ Ruby Private Classes
- ➢ Freezing Objects
- ➢ Inheritance and Encapsulation
- ➢ Polymorphism and Constructors
- ➢ Access Control
- ➢ Mixins
- ➢ Instance Variables
- ➢ Data Abstraction
- ➢ Static Members in Ruby

In the previous chapter, we covered the overview of Ruby, and in this chapter, we will discuss Object-oriented programming (OOP)'s concepts.

OOP means that our code is focused on objects. Objects are real-world examples that may be divided into several kinds.

Consider the example that follows to better understand this. If we take a rose as an object, the class of the rose is flower. A class is comparable to an object's design in that it describes the characteristics and behavior of the

DOI: 10.1201/9781003358510-2

object. A flower's characteristics might include its color, scent, or even the presence of thorns.[1]

These characteristics are part of the class, and each example of the class, that is, each object of the class, would share them. But the property's value may differ between objects. Consider the lily as an instance. So, if the petals of the rose item are red, the lily's petals may be white. This is the foundation of OOP, where we can take real-world circumstances and create various instances from them.

Let's look at how to define a class in Ruby.

Class's syntax:

```
class class_name
end
```

IMPLEMENTATION OF OOP CONCEPTS OF RUBY

By permitting the development of classes and their objects, Ruby supports the OOP paradigm. Objects, as previously said, are instances of a class, and a class serves as the blueprint for the object. A class describes the properties of an item and determines its behavior, whereas the object is its physical embodiment.

A class is made up of two parts: data and methods.

So, now that we have a Language class, let us specify the following characteristics.

1. LanguageName

2. TopicName

We now have our data but need a mechanism to access it. This is when our strategies come into play. Class methods are class-defined methods that are utilized to retrieve various data in our class. To implement into code, we utilize a constructor, which accepts attribute values and assigns them to the area reserved for the specific object.

Syntax of a constructor:

```
def initialize(m, n)
    @m = m
    @n = n
end
```

The initialize function is specified within the class and has the same syntax as any other function. It can withstand any number of arguments. The @ symbol denotes the actual characteristics of the object.

Example:

```
class Languages
    def initialize(languages_name, topics_name)
        @languages_name = languages_name
        @topics_name = topics_name
    end
end
```

To construct a class instance, we utilize a method that we may have used previously to build hashes or arrays. We make advantage of the new function.

Syntax:

```
Object-name  = Class-name.new()
```

If we have parameters, they are often passed in the parentheses of new, exactly like in normal methods.

Example:

```
class Languages
    def initialize(languages_name, topics_name)
        @languages_name = languages_name
        @topics_name = topics_name
    end
end

object1 = Languages.new('Ruby','method')
```

So, we have a named item called object1. To create a new example, we use Languages.new(), which executes the initialize method. As an outcome, the object1.languages_name is Ruby. and method is object1. topics_name.

Let us also make a second item.

Example:

```
class Languages
    def initialize(languages_name, topics_name)
        @languages_name = languages_name
        @topics_name = topics_name
    end
end

object1 = Languages.new('Ruby','method')
object2 = Languages.new('Scala','string')
```

Scala is the object2.languages_name. In addition, object2.topics_name is a string.

Access Methods

We need to be able to alter or inspect the attributes of our object now that we've declared our class and produced objects. This is where the second portion of our class, Methods, comes in. Class methods are similar to normal methods that are defined within a class.

Methods are used to modify the value of certain of our characteristics as well as to see the values. To invoke a specific method, we must use the object_name.method_name syntax. An example will help us understand this better.

Example:

```
# program to understand concept of
# Access Method
class Languages
    def initialize(languages_name, topics_name)
        @languages_name = languages_name
        @topics_name = topics_name
    end

    # Define Methods
    def return_name
        return @languages_name
    end
    def return_topics
        return @topics_name
    end
end
```

```
# Create objects
object1 = Languages.new('Ruby','method')
object2 = Languages.new('Scala','string')
puts 'Languages name for object1: ' + object1
.return_name
puts 'Topics Name for object1: ' + object1
.return_topics

puts 'Languages name for object2: ' + object2
.return_name
puts 'Topics Name for object2: ' + object2
.return_topics
```

In the preceding example, we generated two objects. object1.return_
name invokes the function return_name for object1, returning the value
"Ruby." When we call object2.return_topic, it invokes the object2 function
return_topic. This returns the method result to the puts statement.

Methods in Ruby typically return the method's most recent computing
result, so we don't need to write return explicitly.

Instead of writing the code below,

```
def return-name
    return @vehicle-name
end
```

We can write code like this.

```
def return-name
    @vehicle-name
end
```

Variable Scope

When we say variable scope, we mean the places in which a variable can
utilize. The scope might be both global and local. When we say global, we
imply that we may utilize the global variable everywhere in our code. The
"$" sign is used to define global variables.

Example:

```
# program to understand concept of
# Variable Scope
```

```ruby
class Languages

    # Create global variable
    $reader = 'ABCD'
    def initialize(languages_name, topics_name)
        @languages_name = languages_name
        @topics_name = topics_name
    end

    # Define Methods
    def return_name
        return @languages_name
    end
    def return_topics
        return @topics_name
    end
end

# Create objects
object1 = Languages.new('Ruby','method')
object2 = Languages.new('Scala','string')
puts 'Languages name for object1: ' + object1
.return_name
puts 'Topics Name for object1: ' + object1
.return_topics

puts 'Languages name for object2: ' + object2
.return_name
puts 'Topics Name for object2: ' + object2
.return_topics

# Print global variable
puts 'The reader is '+ $reader
```

We declared a global variable in the preceding example. We may use this variable everywhere in the program since it is global. ABCD is the responsibility of $reader. Let's try it using one of the object1.languages_name instance variables. This would have resulted in an error since this variable has a local scope, meaning it can only be used within the class. As a result, we must utilize access methods or attr_reader, as detailed below.

Changing the Attributes

Let us illustrate with an example.

```ruby
# program to understand concept of
# Modifying attributes
class Languages
def initialize(languages_name, topics_name)
        @languages_name = languages_name
        @topics_name = topics_name
    end

# Define Method
    def return_name
        return @languages_name
    end
    def return_topics
        return @topics_name
    end
    def modify_topics(value)
        @topics_name = value
    end
end

# Create object
object = Languages.new('Ruby','method')
puts 'Languages name for object: '+object.return_name
puts 'Topics name is '+object.return_topics

# Modifying attribute
object.modify_topics('string')
puts 'New Topics Name is '+object.return_topics
```

In the above instance, we observe a new method called modify_topics. This method is used to alter the value of the topics_name property. Because the properties cannot access directly outside the function, we must rely on methods to do so. As seen in the example, we send the new subject to the modify_topics function as an input. The object's subject attribute is reset to the new topic within the function.

Class Variables

Class variables vary from instance variables in that they belong to the class rather than the object. For variables such as languages_name and topics_name, we have one copy for each object, whereas class variables have one copy shared by all objects. The variable normally belongs to the class rather than the instances of the class, although the instances of the class can still access it. "@@" is commonly used to identify class variables. @@class_variable = 0 is the syntax. It can have a default value, anything from a string to an integer.

Example:

```ruby
# program to understand concept of
# Class Variables
class Languages
    $reader = 'ABCD'

    # Create class variable
    @@count = 0
    def initialize(languages_name, topics_name)
        @languages_name = languages_name
        @topics_name = topics_name
        @@count += 1
    end

    # Define method
    def return_name
        @languages_name
    end
    def return_topics
        @topics_name
    end

    # Return class variable
    def return_count
        @@count
    end
end

# Create object
object1 = Languages.new('Ruby', 'method')
object2 = Languages.new('Scala', 'string')
puts 'Languages name for object1: '+object1
.return_name
```

```
puts 'Topics name for object1: '+object1
.return_topics

puts 'Languages name for object2: '+object2
.return_name
puts 'Topics name for object2: '+object2
.return_topics

puts 'The reader is '+ $reader

puts 'Number of objects created is ' + object1
.return_count.to_s
puts 'Number of objects created is ' + object2
.return_count.to_s
```

In the preceding example, we used a class variable count to keep track of the number of objects generated. This is one of the most typical uses of class variables. In the preceding instance, we set count to 0. We also include a function that returns the value when invoked.

When an object is formed, the initialize method is called. Each time the initialize function is run, count is increased by one, that is, @@count += 1 regardless of whether we call the return_count method with object1 or object2. It has the same scope as instance variables and cannot be accessed from outside the class we use. to_s is used to convert a number to a string.

Instead of Access Methods

In the previous examples, we presented methods for returning character-istics. We have a simpler solution. Consider the following code for attr_reader, attr_writer, and attr_accessor.

```
# program to understand concept of
# Modify attributes
class Languages
        attr_reader :languages_name
        attr_writer :topics_name
        attr_reader :topics_name

    def initialize(languages_name, topics_name)
            @languages_name = languages_name
            @topics_name = topics_name
    end

end
```

```
object = Languages.new('Ruby', 'method')
puts 'The name of the languages is ' + object
.languages_name
puts 'The topics of the languages is ' + object
.topics_name

# change the topics name
object.topics_name = 'array'
puts 'The new topics of the language is ' + object
.topics_name
```

Inheritance

One of the essential features of OOP is inheritance. Certain characteristics of one class may need to be duplicated in another. Instead of defining that attribute from scratch, we may inherit it from another class. The class inherited from is known as the base class, and the class inherited from the base class is known as the derived class.[2]

Syntax:

```
class Class_base
# internal data and methods
end
class Class_derived < base
# internal data and methods
end
```

For inheritance, we utilize the < symbol. As a result, the derived class inherits all of the data and methods from the base class. However, this is simply one option. That is, the data from the derived class is not sent back to the base class. This is simpler to grasp with an illustration, so consider our basic example Vehicle.

Let's start with the base class Vehicle and create two derived classes: car and bus.

Example:

```
# program of Inheritance
class Vehicles
    def initialize(vehicles_name, vehicles_color)
        @vehicles_name = vehicles_name
```

```ruby
        @vehicles_color = vehicles_color
    end
    def descriptions
        puts 'This is vehicle'
    end
end

class Car < Vehicle
    def descriptions
        puts 'This is car'
    end

end

class Bus < Vehicle
    def display_this
        puts 'This is bus'
    end

end

# Create objects
object1 = Car.new('BMW', 'red')
object2 = Bus.new('Volvo', 'grey')

object1.descriptions
object2.descriptions
object2.display_this
```

In the above example, there is one base class, Vehicles, and two derived classes, Car and Bus. Car and Bus inherit the characteristics and methods of the class Vehicles, with the exception of the method "Descriptions," which is shared by both Vehicles and Car, although their usefulness differs. So, when Car inherits the methods from Vehicles, it has two methods called Descriptions, but they are not the same; one is Car.Descriptions and the other is Vehicles.Descriptions.

When we call the Descriptions method on a Car object, the Car.Descriptions method is executed.

As a result, we can argue that Car.Descriptions takes precedence over Vehicles.Descriptions. There is only one Descriptions method in the Bus class, which we inherited from the vehicles' class; therefore, there is no overriding in this situation. The method "display_this" is an example of a derived class with its own data and variables. Remember that inheritance does not work the other way around.

So, if we had an object of type Vehicles, for example, object3 = Vehicles. new(), we couldn't write object3.display_this since inheritance is just one way.

Examine the two Description methods, "Car.descriptions" and "Vehicles. Descriptions." We declare that for a Car object, the Car.Descriptions method will be called, but what if we wanted the other method-Vehicles. Descriptions to be used? To do this, we employ the keyword super.

```ruby
# program of inheritance
class Vehicles
    def initialize(vehicles_name, vehicles_color)
        @vehicles_name = vehicles_name
        @vehicles_color = vehicles_color
    end
    def descriptions
        puts 'This is vehicle'
    end
end

# Use inheritance
class Car < Vehicles
    def descriptions
        puts 'This is car'
            super
    end

end

# Use inheritance
class Bus < Vehicles
    def display_this
        puts 'This is bus'
    end

end

# create object
object1 = Car.new('BMW', 'red')
object2 = Bus.new('Volvo', 'grey')
```

```
# Call object
object1.descriptions
object2.descriptions
object2.display_this
```

The difference between this and the previous instance is that we utilize super in the Car.Descriptions function. When we use super, the control returns to the base class and performs the base class method, that is, Vehicles.Descriptions rather than Car.Descriptions.

This is how we may override our derived class method and replace it with our base class method.

Derived Class Attributes

Assume we want our derived class to have its own set of attributes. We would still need to pass the variables for both the base and derived classes. The constructor of the base class is then called using super, and the attributes of the derived class are initialized.

Example:

```
# program of displaying Derived class attributes
class Vehicles
    attr_accessor :vehicles_name
    attr_accessor :vehicles_color
    def initialize(vehicles_name, vehicles_color)
        @vehicles_name = vehicles_name
        @vehicles_color = vehicles_color
    end
end

class Car < Vehicles
    attr_accessor :car_model
def initialize(vehicles_name, vehicles_color,
car_model)

        # Use super keyword
        super(vehicles_name, vehicles_color)
        @car_model = car_model
    end
end
```

```
# create object
object = Car.new('BMW', 'white', 'abc')

# call object
puts object.vehicles_name
puts object.vehicles_color
puts object.car_model
```

In the derived class, we added the attribute car_model. While creating the object, we supplied values for both the base and derived class (Car), as the derived class has the properties of both the base and derived class (Vehicles).

Object = Car.new("BMW," "white," "abc") The control is passed to the Car's initialize function, and then we use super to provide the Vehicles attributes to the Vehicles' initialize method, that is, super(vehicles_name, vehicles_color). The control is then passed into the vehicles initialize function before returning to where it was called. The derived attributes are then initialized, that is, @car_model = car_model.

Multiple inheritances are not enabled in Ruby because it may quickly become chaotic and difficult. Multiple inheritances mean that one class is descended from several base classes. Languages such as C++ enable this; however, it is frequently regarded as overcomplicated. We do, however, have a workaround for this. Mixins can generally assist to compensate for this shortage.

Public and Private

By default, all of our attributes and methods are public. If we describe all of our methods as public, it enables our methods to be accessible outside the class. If we define all of our methods as private, only the object is allowed access to utilize the methods internally from other public methods.

```
# program of Public and Private method
class Vehicles
    def initialize(vehicles_name, vehicles_color)
        @vehicles_name = vehicles_name
        @vehicles_color = vehicles_color
    end

# Use public method
    public
```

```
    def displays
        greeting
        puts 'Our car details are: '
        puts @vehicles_name
        puts @vehicles_color
    end

# Use Private method
    private
    def greeting
        puts 'Hey, user'
    end
end

# Create object
object = Vehicles.new('BMW', 'white')

# Call object
object.displays
```

All of our methods are public by default, so if we want one of them to be private, we must specify it with the term private. Similarly, we may refer to a method as public by using the term as public. If we use one of the keywords private or public, it will remain in that state until we mention it again at the end of the class definition.

Modules

Modules are blocks of code that include methods and even constants. When coding, we may have a lot of tools that we want to utilize, but this may clog up the entire program. So we place things in modules and only utilize the modules when we want to use the methods and constants within. Modules are identical to classes with the difference that they cannot use to build objects.

Syntax of module:

```
module Module_Name
    #methods and constants
end
```

Module names are written in CapitalizedCamelCase, which simply capitalizes the first letter of each word in the module name with no spaces.

Example:

```
module Constants&Methods
    CONST_ONE = 20
    CONST_TWO = 30

    def method1
        puts 'This belongs to the
Constants&Methods'
    end
end
```

Constants&Methods is a module that we designed. There are two constants. Constants should be expressed in capital letters with underscores between words, and we have a method named method1. The keyword require is used to access data and methods within a module. The constants and methods can then be accessed using the scope resolution operator.

```
require 'Constants&Methods'

puts Constants&Methods::CONST_ONE
```

We'll continue our introduction to modules by learning about mixins.

Mixins

Mixins are our crossover among modules and classes, and they are how we get around Ruby's restriction on multiple inheritance. Using the term include, we may include our modules' constants and methods in our classes.

Example:

```
# program of using mixins
module Greetings
    def displays
        puts 'Hello'
    end
end

class Greetuser
    include Greetings
    attr_reader :name
```

```
        def initialize(name)
            @name = name
        end
end

# Creat object
object = Greetuser.new('User-name')

# Call object
object.displays
puts object.name
```

We have a module called Greetings and a class called Greetuser. As we can see in this line object.show, we are utilizing the Greetuser object to call the module function display. We can implement this because of the include we performed in class, specifically include Greetings.

Extend Mixins

Instead, we may use extend. The distinction is that extend integrates the module at the class level, thus the class itself can utilize the module methods rather than objects.

Example:

```
# program of extending mixins
module Greetings
    def displays
        puts 'Hello'
    end
end

# Use extend keyword
class Greetuser
    extend Greetings
attr_reader :name
    def initialize(name)
        @name = name
    end
end

# Create object
object = Greetuser.new('User-name')
```

```
# Call object
Greetuser.displays
puts object.name
```

In the preceding example, include was substituted with extend. So, it's now officially part of the class. As a result, we may utilize the module's function with the class name Greetuser.display.

CLASSES AND OBJECTS IN RUBY

Ruby is an outstanding Object-oriented language of programming. An OOP language has characteristics such as data encapsulation, polymorphism, inheritance, data abstraction, operator overloading, and so on. Classes and objects are crucial in OOP.[3]

A class is a template from which objects can build. An object is also known as a class instance. For instance, mammals, birds, fish, reptiles, and amphibians are all examples of the class animal. Similarly, the class is the sales department, and the objects of the class are sales data, sales manager, and secretary.

Defining a Class in Ruby

Classes and objects may be readily defined with Ruby. Simply type the class keyword followed by the class name. The initial letter of the class name must capitalize.[4]

Syntax:

```
class Class-name

end
```

The end keyword terminates a class, and all data members are located between the class declaration and the end keyword.

Example:

```
# class name is Animals
class Animals

# class variables
@@type_of_animals = 5
@@no_of_animals = 4

end
```

Creating Objects in Ruby with the "New" Method

Ruby's most significant components are classes and objects. Like class objects, we may generate a large number of objects from a single class. The new method in Ruby is used to create objects.

Syntax:

```
Object-name = Class-name.new
```

Example:

```
# class name is box
class Box

# class variable
@@No_of_color = 4

end

# Two Objects of the Box class
sbox = Box.new
nbox = Box.new
```

Box is the class's name, and No_of_color is the class's variable. The box class has two objects: sbox and nbox. (=) is followed by the class name, the dot operator, and the new method.

Method Definition in Ruby

In Ruby, member functions are referred to as methods. A method name follows the def keyword to declare each method. The method name is always in lowercase, and the method concludes with the end keyword. Each class and method in Ruby ends with the keyword end.

Syntax:

```
def method-name

# statements or code to execute

end
```

Example:

```ruby
# program to illustrate
# define of methods

#!/usr/bin/ruby

# define class Vehicles
class PFP

# define method
def peeks

# print result
puts "Hello Peeks!"

# end of method
end

# end of class PFP
end

# create object
obj = PFP.new

# call method using object
obj.peeks
```

Passing Parameters to the New Method

The user can supply any number of parameters to the "new method," which are used to initialize the class variables. When passing arguments to "new method," it is necessary to specify an initialize method at the time of class construction. The initialize method is a specific method that is executed when the new method with parameters is triggered.

Example:

```ruby
# program to illustrate passing
# parameters to new method

#!/usr/bin/ruby
```

```
# define class Vehicle
class Vehicles

# initialize method
def initialize(id, color, name)

# variables
@veh-id = id
@veh-color = color
@veh-name = name

# displaying values
puts "ID is: #@veh-id"
puts "Color is: #@veh-color"
puts "Name is: #@veh-name"
puts "\n"
end
end

# Create objects and passing parameters
# to new method
xveh = Vehicles. new("1", "Blue", "PQR")
yveh = Vehicles. new("2", "Grey", "ABC")
```

Explanation: The class name in this case is Vehicle. In Ruby, the keyword def is used to define the "initialize" method. When a new object is formed, it calls this method. When the new class method is invoked, it always calls the initialize instance method. The initialize function is similar to a constructor in that it is called whenever new objects are created. The arguments in the initialize method are id, color, and name, and the local variables in the initialize method are @veh_id, @veh_color, and @veh_name. Using these local variables, we sent the value along the new method. The arguments in the "new" method are always surrounded by double quotes.

PRIVATE CLASSES IN RUBY

The idea of private, protected, and public methods in Ruby differs from that of other languages such as Java.[5]

Because classes are objects in Ruby, it only matters which class the person is calling.

Private Class

When a constant in Ruby is marked private, it signifies that it can never be called with an explicit recipient; instead, a private constant can only be called with an implicit receiver. So, in Ruby, private classes may be defined within a class as a subclass and declared as private constants; this private class can only be accessible via the outer-class.

Syntax:

```
Private-constant: class
```

Example:

```
# by default public
class Marvels

# by default public
class Guardians
    def Quill
        puts "Legendary outlaw"
        end
    def Groot
        puts "I am a Groot"
        end
    end

# by default public
class Avengers
    def Tony
        puts "I am a Iron-man"
    end
    end
end
Marvels::Avengers.new.Tony
Marvels::Guardians.new.Quill
```

Because the subclasses Guardians and Avengers are public in the above instance, both implicit and explicit users have access to them.

- Look into the private class.

Example:

```
# program of accessing private class
# public
class Marvels

# Private
class Guardians
    def Quill
        puts "Legendary outlaw"
        end
    def Groot
        puts "I am a Groot"
        end
    end

# public
class Avengers
    def Tony
        puts "I am a Iron-man"
    end
    end

# making Guardians class private
private_constant :Guardians
end

Marvels::Avengers.new.Tony

# throws an error(NameError)
Marvels::Guardians.new.Quill
```

So, the program has no access-specifier keywords to make a class private or public, although they exist in Ruby but cannot deal with classes. To make a class private, use the private constant function. This function makes any object, class, or method private, making it inaccessible to explicit users.

How may a private class be accessible via the outer-class?

```
# program a private class accessed through
outer-class.
# public
```

```ruby
class Marvels

# private
class Guardians
    def Quill
        puts "Legendary outlaw"
        end
    def Groot
        puts "I am a Groot"
        end
    end

# private
class Avengers
    def Tony
        puts "I am a Iron-man"
    end
    end

# the outer-class method accessing private classes
def fury
    Guardians.new.Groot
    Avengers.new.Tony
end
private_constant :Guardians
private_constant :Avengers
end

# calls fury method in the Marvels call.
Marvel.new.fury

# throws error as it is explicit accessing.
Marvels::Avengers.new.Tony

# throws error as it is explicit accessing.
Marvels::Guardians.new.Quill
```

The private class (inner-class) can only be accessed through its outer-class. And private classes can only exist as inner-class alone. As seen in the above code, we accessed Groot and Tony (private class methods) using fury (outer-class method) by constructing Guardians.new and Avengers.new (private class objects) and calling the relevant methods with the respective objects Guardians.new.Groot and Avengers.new. Tony from wrath (calling the tactics) (outer-class method). If the outer-class is private, both implicit and explicit users cannot access it because it is not feasible to create an object for a private class outside of its class. As a result, no access.

FREEZING OBJECTS IN RUBY

Object#freeze may use to freeze any object. A frozen object cannot alter: we cannot change its instance variables, we cannot connect singleton methods with it, and we cannot add, delete, or edit its methods if it is a class or module.[6]

Object#frozen may be used to determine whether an object is frozen. If the object is frozen, it returns true; else, it returns false. Using the freeze method in an object, we may convert an object into a constant.

It should note that a frozen object cannot unfreeze.[7]

Syntax:

```
Object-Name.freeze
```

Example:

```
# program of freezing object

# define class
class Addition
# constructor method
def initialize(x, y)
    @m, @n = x, y
end

# accessor methods
def getM
    @m
end
def getN
    @n
end

# setter methods
def setM=(value)
    @m = value
```

```
end
def setN=(value)
    @n = value
end
end

# create object
add = Addition.new(20, 30)

# let us freeze this object
add.freeze
if( add.frozen? )
puts "The Addition object is frozen object"
else
puts "The Addition object is normal object"
end

# now try using setter methods
add.setM = 40
add.setN = 60

# use accessor methods
add.getM()
add.getN()

puts "M is : #{add.getM()}"
puts "N is : #{add.getN()}"
```

In the above instance, we establish a class called Addition, and then we construct an object called add. We can't modify the value of the object's method since we used the add.freeze method. The add.frozen? function is used to determine if the item is frozen or not.

INHERITANCE IN RUBY

Ruby is the ideal OOP language. Inheritance is one of the most essential qualities of an object-oriented machine code. Inheritance enables a programmer to pass on the attributes of one class to another. Ruby only allows single-class inheritance; it does not support multiple-class inheritance; however, it does support mixins. The mixins are intended to implement multiple inheritances in Ruby, although just the interface component is inherited.[8]

Inheritance introduces the idea of "reusability," which means that if a programmer wants to construct a new class and there is an existing class that already has part of the code that the coder needs, the programmer can derive a new class from the current class. This enhances the reuse of the current class's fields and functions without adding new code.

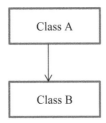

Base class and Drive class.

Class A is the superclass in the above illustration, while class B is a subclass, or class B is derived from class A (Base Class).

Inheritance Terminology

Superclass: A superclass, base class, or parent class is the class whose attributes are inherited.

Subclass: A class that is derived from another class is referred to as a subclass, derived class, or child class. In addition to basic class methods and objects, we may add our own objects and methods.[9]

Every class in Ruby has a parent class by default. Prior to Ruby 1.9, the Object class was the parent class of all other classes, or the root of the class hierarchy. However, as of Ruby 1.9, the BasicObject class is the super class (parent class) of all other Ruby classes. The Object class is a subclass of the BasicObject class.

Syntax:

```
Subclass-name < superclass-name
```

Example:

```
# program to demonstrate
# the Inheritance

#!/usr/bin/ruby
```

```ruby
# Super class or parent class
class PeeksforPeeks

    # constructor of the super class
    def initialize

        puts "This is the Superclass"
    end

    # method of superclass
    def supermethod

        puts "Method of the superclass"
    end
end

# subclass or derived class
class SudoPlacement < PeeksforPeeks

    # constructor of deriver class
    def initialize

    puts "This is Subclass"
    end
end

# creating object of the superclass
PeeksforPeeks.new

# creating object of subclass
subobj = SudoPlacement.new

# calling method of super
# class using the sub class object
Subobj.supermethod
```

Overriding a Parent or Superclass Method

Ruby's method overriding is a powerful feature. Method overriding occurs when a subclass and a superclass share the same method name but execute distinct duties, or when one method overrides another. If both the superclass and the subclass have the same method name, the subclass method will be run.

Example:

```
# program to demonstrate
# Overriding of Parent or
# Superclass method

#!/usr/bin/ruby

# parent class
class Peeks

    # method of superclass
    def supermethod

        puts "This is the Superclass Method"
end

end

# derived class 'Ruby'
class Ruby < Peeks

    # overriding the method of superclass
    def supermethod

        puts "Override by the Subclass"
end
end

# creating object of the sub class
obj = Ruby.new

# calling method
obj.supermethod
```

Inheritance Using the Super Method

Inheritance uses the super method to invoke the parent class method from the child class. If the method does not have any parameters, it immediately passes all of them. The super keyword defines a super method. We may just type super or super whenever we wish to invoke a parent class method of the same name ().

Example:

```ruby
# Program to demonstrate the
# use of the super method

#!/usr/bin/ruby

# base class
class Peeks_1

    # method of the superclass accepting
    # two parameter
    def display a = 0, b = 0
        puts "Parent class, 1st Argument: #{a},
2nd Argument: #{b}"
    end
end

# derived class Peeks_2
class Peeks_2 < Peeks_1

    # subclass method having same name
    # as the superclass
    def display a, b

        # calling superclass method
        # by default it will pass
        # both arguments
        super

        # passing only one argument
        super a

        # passing both argument
        super a, b

        # calling the superclass method
        # by default it will not pass
        # both the arguments
        super()

        puts "Hey! This is the subclass method"
    end
```

```
end

# creating object of the derived class
obj = Peeks_2.new

# calling method of subclass
obj.display "Sudo_Placement", "PFP"
```

POLYMORPHISM IN RUBY

Variable types are not available in Ruby, as they are in other programming languages. Every variable is an "object" that may be updated separately. Every object may easily have methods and functions added to it. OOP, therefore, plays a significant role in this case. Inheritance, encapsulation, and other foundations of object-oriented programming may be found in any other computer language.[10] Polymorphism is one of these pillars.

Polymorphism is derived from the terms poly, which means many, and morph, which means forms. Polymorphism is a way in which the same procedure may be executed using various objects. Polymorphism allows us to get multiple results from the same function by giving different input items. If-else commands can also be written; however, this increases the length of the code. To circumvent this, programmers devised the notion of polymorphism.

Classes in polymorphism have separate functionality but have common interference. The idea of polymorphism may be broken down into several subcategories.

- Polymorphism using inheritance

- Polymorphism using duck-typing

Polymorphism Using Inheritance

Inheritance is a property that allows a child class to inherit a parent class's attributes and methods. Polymorphism may be readily implemented via inheritance. It is best illustrated with the following example:

```
# program of Polymorphism using the inheritance
class Vehicles
    def tyreType
        puts "Heavy Cars"
    end
end
```

```ruby
# Using the inheritance
class Cars < Vehicles
    def tyreType
        puts "Small Cars"
    end
end

# Using the inheritance
class Trucks < Vehicles
    def tyreType
        puts "Big Cars"
    end
end

# Create object
vehicles = Vehicles.new
vehicles.tyreType()

# Create different object calling the same function
vehicles = Cars.new
vehicles.tyreType()

# Create different object calling the same function
vehicles = Trucks.new
vehicles.tyreType()
```

The program above is a very easy method of performing basic polymorphism. The tyreType function is called using various objects such as Cars and Trucks. The Cars and Trucks classes are both subclasses of Vehicles. Both inherit the methods of the vehicles' class (primarily the tyreType method).

Polymorphism Using Duck-Typing

In Ruby, we concentrate on the abilities and characteristics of the object rather than its class. So, duck-typing is just focusing on the concept of what an item can do rather than what it is. Alternatively, what actions might be done on the object rather than the object's class?

Here is a simple code that depicts the previously described method.

```ruby
# program of polymorphism using Duck typing

# Create three different classes
class Hotels
```

```ruby
def enters
    puts "Customers enters"
end

def type(customers)
    customers.type
end

def rooms(customers)
    customers.room
end

end

# Create class with the two methods
class Single

def type
    puts "Room is on fourth floor."
end

def rooms
    puts "Per night stay is five thousand"
end

end

class Couples

# Same methods as in class single
def type
    puts "Room is on second floor"
end

def rooms
    puts "Per night stay is eight thousand"
end

end

# Create Object
# Performing polymorphism
```

```
hotels= Hotels.new
puts "This visitor is Single."
customers = Single.new
hotels.type(customers)
hotels.room(customers)

puts "Visitors are couples."
customers = Couples.new
hotels.type(customers)
hotels.room(customers)
```

In the preceding example, the customer object is involved in interacting with the customer's characteristics such as its "type" and "rooms." Polymorphism is demonstrated here.

CONSTRUCTORS IN RUBY

A constructor is a class method that is automatically called whenever a new instance of the class is created. A constructor, like methods, may include a collection of instructions or a procedure that will be executed when the object is created.[11]

Important considerations for constructors:

- Constructors are used to set up instance variables.

- Unlike in most computer languages, the constructor in Ruby has a distinct name.

- The initialize and def keywords are used to define a constructor.

- Ruby treats it as a unique method.

- In Ruby, constructors can be overloaded.

- Constructors cannot be passed down.

- It returns the class's instance.

Note: When a class object is created using the new method, it internally executes the initialize function on the new object. Furthermore, all arguments provided to new are immediately sent to method initialize.

Syntax:

```
class Class-Name
```

```
    def initialize(parameter-list)

    end

end
```

Example:

```
# program to demonstrate
# working of constructor

#!/usr/bin/ruby

# class name1
class Demo1

    # constructor
    def initialize
        puts "Welcome to PeeksforPeeks!"
    end

end

# Create Object
Demo1.new
```

Instance Variable Initialization

Instance variables may be initialized using the constructor. The constructor provides the initial value to instance variables, which may then be utilized everywhere in the code.[12]

Example:

```
# program to initialize instance
# variable using the constructor

#!/usr/bin/ruby

# class name1
class Peeks

    # constructor
```

```ruby
    def initialize

        # instance variable initialization
        @inst_1 = "PeeksforPeeks"
        @inst_2 = "Sudo Placement"
    end

    # display method
    def display
        puts "Value of the First instance variable
is: #{@inst_1}"
        puts "Value of the Second instance
variable is: #{@inst_2}"
    end
end

# create object
objt = Peeks.new()

# call display method
objt.display()
```

ACCESS CONTROL IN RUBY

Access control is a critical component of OOP languages that is used to limit the accessibility of methods and member fields in order to safeguard data from unintentional alteration. Ruby differs from all other object-oriented computer languages in terms of access control.[13]

Critical Ruby access control considerations:

- The class variable and instance's visibility are always private.

- Methods are the only ones that have access restrictions.

- We can't restrict access to the instance and class variables.

- Private methods in Ruby, like public and protected methods, can be inherited.

Access control in Ruby works on two conditions:

- First, consider if the method is called from within or outside of the class definition.

- Second, whether or not the self-keyword is included. Essentially, self-keyword is employed to direct attention to the current receiver.

In Ruby, inheritance does not need to require access control; however, in C++, access control is used in inheritance. There are three different types of access control, as shown in the following figure.

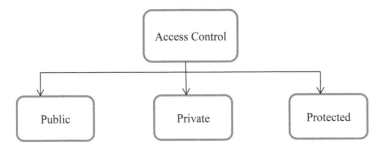

Types of access control.

Public Method

Public methods are ones that may be accessed by anybody. Because access control only works on methods, all methods are public by default. However, we may explicitly specify a public method by using the public keyword. Outside of the class, public methods are often called.

Example:

```
# program to demonstrate the
# public access control

#!/usr/bin/ruby

# take a class
class PeeksforPeeks

    # public method without using
    # the public keyword
    def peeks_1
        puts "public method peeks_1 is called"
    end

    # using public keyword
```

```
    public

    def peeks_2
        puts "public method peeks_2 is called"
    end

    def peeks_3

        puts "public method peeks_3 is called"

        # calling peeks_1 method
        peeks_1

        # calling peeks_1 method using
        # self-keyword
        self.peeks_1
    end
end

# create the object of
# class PeeksforPeeks
obj = PeeksforPeeks.new

# calling method peeks_1
obj.peeks_1

# calling method peeks_2
obj.peeks_2

# calling method peeks3
obj.peeks_3
```

Private Method

Private methods are those that are not available outside of the class; in other words, private methods are only referred to within the class declaration. The class's methods have access to secret members. We do not utilize the self-keyword in private methods. The initialize function is a private method by default. The initialize method cannot be made public by the user. The private keyword is used to declare a private method.[14]

Private methods, as we know, are strongly limited in terms of visibility; only defined class members can access these methods, but they can be inherited by the subclass. They can be accessed and overridden by a subclass.

Example:

```ruby
# program to demonstrate the
# private access control

#!/usr/bin/ruby

# create class
class PeeksforPeeks

    # using the initialize method
    # it can't private
    def initialize
        puts "This is initialize Method"
    end

    # public method
    def peeks_1

            puts "Public peeks_1 Method"
        end

    # using private keyword to
    # declare a private method
    private

    def peeks_2

        puts "This is a Private Method"
    end

end

# create the object of
# the class PeeksforPeeks
obj = PeeksforPeeks.new

# calling method peeks_1
# (peeks1 method is public method)
```

```
obj.peeks_1

# calling private method will give error
obj.peeks_2
```

Protected Method

Only objects of the given class and its subclasses can invoke protected methods. The access to these methods is restricted to the declared class or its subclass. Outside of the declared class or its subclass, you cannot access protected methods. The use of secured techniques is limited. The protected keyword is used to specify protected methods.

Example:

```
# program to demonstrate
# protected access control

#!/usr/bin/ruby

class PeeksforPeeks

    # using the initialize method
    def initialize

        # calling peeks_2 method
        peeks_2

        # calling peeks_2 method
        # using self-keyword
        self.peeks_2

    end

    # public method
    def peeks_1
        puts " peeks_1 method is called"
    end

    # defining protected method using
    # protected keyword
    protected
```

```
    def peeks_2
        puts " peeks_2 method is called"
    end

end

# create the object of class PeeksforPeeks
obj = PeeksforPeeks.new

# calling method
obj.peeks_1

# if we will try to call protected method
# using object of class then it will
# give error
obj.peeks_2
```

Notes:

- On the inside of a public method of the same class, the user can invoke the private and protected methods.

   Example:

```
# program to demonstrate the calling
# of private and protected method in
# the public method

class Peeks

    # public method
    def method_1

    p "Public Method of class Peeks"

        # call protected and private method
        # inside public method
        method_2
        method_3
    end

    # define the protected method
    protected
```

```
        def method_2

            p "Protected Method of class Peeks"
        end

        # define the private method
        private

        def method_3

        p "Private Method of class Peeks"

        end
    end

    # creating an object of class Peeks
    obj = Peeks.new

    # calling the public method of class Peeks
    obj.method_1
```

- In most object-oriented computer languages, private methods cannot be inherited. Private methods, like protected and public methods, can inherite in Ruby.

Example:

```
# program to demonstrate that private
# method can also inherite

class Peeks

    # public method
    def method_1

        p "Public Method of class Peeks"

    end

    # define the protected method
    protected

    def method_2
```

```ruby
        p "Protected Method of class Peeks"
    end

    # define the private method
    private

    def method_3

        p "Private Method of class Peeks"

    end
end

# Sudo class inheriting Peeks class
class Sudo < Peeks

    # public method of the Sudo class
    def method_4

        p "Public Method of the Sudo Class"

        # call all three methods
        # of Peeks class
        method_1
        method_2
        method_3
    end
end

# create an object of class Sudo
obj_sudo = Sudo.new

# call the public method
# of the class Sudo which will
# automatically call private
# and protected method of Peeks class
obj_sudo.method_4
```

- Outside of the class in which they are declared, public methods can be accessed. However, outside of the class in which they were declared, the user cannot access the private and protected methods.

Example:

```ruby
# program to demonstrate that private
# and protected method can't access
# outside the class even after the inheritance

class Peeks

    # public method
    def method_1

        p "Public Method of class Peeks"

    end

    # define the protected method
    protected

    def method_2

        p "Protected Method of class Peeks"
    end

    # define the private method
    private

    def method_3

        p "Private Method of class Peeks"

    end
end

# Sudo class inheriting Peeks class
class Sudo < Peeks

    # public method of the Sudo class
    def method_4

        p "Public Method of the Sudo Class"

    end
end
```

```
# create an object of class Sudo
obj_sudo = Sudo.new

# call the public method
# of class Sudo and Peeks
obj_sudo.method_4
obj_sudo.method_1

# if you will try to call protected
# and private method using  object
# of the class Sudo, then it will give error
obj_sudo.method_2
obj_sudo.method_3
```

- The primary distinction between protected and private methods is that protected methods may access from within the class by employing an explicit receiver, but private methods cannot.

Example:

```
# program to demonstrate that private
# and protected method can't access
# outside the class even after the inheritance

class Peeks

    # public method
    def method_1

        p "Public Method of class Peeks"

    end

    # define the protected method
    protected

    def method_2

        p "Protected Method of class Peeks"
    end

    # define the private method
    private

    def method_3
```

```ruby
        p "Private Method of class Peeks"

    end
end

# Sudo class inheriting Peeks class
class Sudo < Geeks

    # public method of the Sudo class
    def method_4

        p "Public Method of the Sudo Class"



        # call the public method
        # of Peeks class
        method_1

        # create object of class Sudo
        # inside public method of
        # class Sudo
        obj_inside_sudo = Sudo.new

        # call the protected
        # method of class Peeks
        obj_inside_sudo.method_2

        # call the private
        # method of class Peeks
        # using explicit receiver
        obj_inside_sudo.method_3 rescue p "We
can't Access!"



    end
end


# create an object of the class Sudo
obj_sudo = Sudo.new

# call the public method
# of class Sudo
obj_sudo.method_4
```

- We may use the following syntax to declare many protected and private methods in a single class:

```
class class-name

   # this method is public
   def public-method
   end

   public :method-1

   protected :method-2, :method-3

   private :method-4, :method-5

end
```

ENCAPSULATION IN RUBY

Encapsulation is the process of enclosing data in a single unit. It is the mechanism that connects code with the data that it manipulates. Encapsulation, on the other hand, is a protective shield that stops programs from accessing data outside of the shield.[15]

- Officially, under encapsulation, a class's variables or data are concealed from other classes and can only be accessible by any member function of the class in which they are specified.[16]

- Encapsulation is performed by designating all variables in the class as private and writing public methods in the class to set and obtain variable values.

Encapsulation

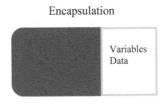

Class

Encapsulation in Ruby.

Example:

```ruby
# program to illustrate encapsulation
#!/usr/bin/ruby

class Demo_encapsulation

def initialize(id, name, addr)

# Instance Variables
@cust-id = id
@cust-name = name
@cust-addr = addr
end

# displaying result
def display-details()
puts "Customer id: #@cust-id"
puts "Customer name: #@cust-name"
puts "Customer address: #@cust-addr"
end
end

# Create Objects
cust1 = Demo_encapsulation. new("1", "Micky",
          "Wisdom Apartments, Delhi")

cust2 = Demo_encapsulation. new("2", "Jatin",
          "New Empire road, Jalandhar")

# Call Methods
cust1.display_details()
cust2.display_details()
```

Explanation: In the preceding code, the class Demo_encapsulation encapsulates the class's methods. These methods can only be accessed with objects from the Demo_encapsulation class, namely, cust1 and cust2.

Benefits of Encapsulation

- *Data hiding*: The user will be ignorant of the internal implementation of the class. The user cannot see how the class keeps values in variables. They just know that the values are being sent to a setter method and that variables are being initialized with that value.

- *Reusability*: Encapsulation promotes reusability and makes it simple to adapt to new requirements.

- *It is simple to test code*: Encapsulated code is simple to unit test.

MIXINS IN RUBY

Before we begin studying Ruby Mixins, we need be familiar with object-oriented concepts. If not, check over object-oriented concepts in Ruby. A class is said to have multiple inheritance when it may inherit characteristics from more than one parent class. However, Ruby does not natively handle multiple inheritance and instead use a tool known as mixin. In Ruby, mixins allow modules to access instance methods of other modules using the include method.[17]

Mixins allow for the controlled addition of functionality to classes. The code in the mixin begins interacting with the code in the class. Mixins are pieces of code wrapped up in a module that a class can include or extend in Ruby. A class is made up of numerous mixins.

First example:

```
# program of mixins

# module consist 2 methods
module P
    def p1
end
def p2
end
end

# module consist 2 methods
module PFP
def pfp1
end
def pfp2
end
end

# Create a class
class PeeksforPeeks
include P
```

```
include PFP
def s1
end
end

# Create object
gfg = PeeksforPeeks.new

# Call methods
pfp.p1
pfp.p2
pfp.pfp1
pfp.pfp2
pfp.s1
```

Module P is made up of the methods p1 and p2. Module PFP includes the methods pfp1 and pfp2. Modules P and PFP are both included in the class PeeksforPeeks. All four methods, namely, p1, p2, pfp1, and pfp2, are accessible to the class PeeksforPeeks. As a result, we can see that the class PeeksforPeeks derives from both modules. As a result, we may argue that the class PeeksforPeeks exhibits mixin.[18]

Second example:

```
# Modules consist method
module Child_1
def c1
puts 'This is the Child one.'
end
end
module Child_2
def c2
puts 'This is the Child two.'
end
end
module Child_3
def c3
puts 'This is the Child three.'
end
end

# Create class
```

```
class Parent
include Child_1
include Child_2
include Child_3
def display
puts 'Three modules have included.'
end
end

# Create object
object = Parent.new

# Call methods
object.display
object.c1
object.c2
object.c3
```

In the above code, module Child 1 contains the method c1. Similarly, Child 2 and Child 3 modules contain the methods c2 and c3. Modules Child 1, Child 2, and Child 3 are part of the Parent class. A method display is also included in the Parent class. As we've seen, the Parent class inherits from all three modules. The Parent class displays multiple inheritance or mixin.

INSTANCE VARIABLES IN RUBY

In Ruby, variables are classified into four types: local variables, instance variables, class variables, and global variables. In Ruby, an instance variable has a name that begins with the @ symbol, and its content is limited to anything that the object itself references to. Even though two objects belong to the same class, they might have distinct values for their instance variables.[19]

Instance variables in Ruby have the following features:

- Before initialization, the instance variable has the value nil.

- By default, all instance variables are private.

- The instance variables of an object can only be accessed through the object's instance methods.

- Ruby instance variables are not required to be declared. This means that the object structure is adaptable.

- When an object is initially referenced, every instance variable is dynamically attached to it.

- An instance variable relates to the object (each object has its own instance variable of that specific class). One example object can change the values of its instance variables without affecting any other instances.

- Except when the method is regarded static, an Instance variable can be utilized by numerous class methods.

Example:

```ruby
# program to illustrate instance variables using
the constructor

class Peek

    # constructor
    def initialize()

        # instance variable
        @peekName = "R2J"
    end

    # define method displayDetails
    def displayDetails()
        puts "Peek name is #@peekName"
    end

end

# create an object of class Peeks
obj=Peek.new()

# call the instance methods of class Peeks
obj.displayDetails()
```

In the preceding example, peekName is an instance variable that was created with a constructor and is accessible by the class Peek's instance function displayDetails().

Let's have a look at another instance to see how instance variables are used in Ruby:

```
# program to illustrate instance variables using the
instance methods

class Peek

    # define instance method getAge
    def getAge(n)

        # instance variable
        @peekAge = n
    end

    # define instance method incrementAge
    def incrementAge()
        @peekAge +=1
    end

    # define instance method displayDetails
    def displayDetails()
        puts "Peek age is #@peekAge"
    end

end

# create an object of class Peeks
obj = Peek.new

# call the instance methods of class Peeks
obj.getAge(22)
obj.displayDetails()
obj.incrementAge()
obj.displayDetails()
```

In the preceding code, peekAge is the instance variable that is initialized in the instance method getAge(). PeekAge is also accessed by the other two instance methods incrementAge() and displayDetails(), where incrementAge() modifies the value of peekAge and displayDetails() displays the value of peekAge.

DATA ABSTRACTION IN RUBY

Data abstraction refers to the concept of expressing relevant features while obscuring functional aspects. This coding method separates the interface from the implementation. Data abstraction is another characteristic of OOP. Abstraction attempts to reduce information so that the developer may focus on a few concepts at a time. The cornerstone of software development is abstraction.[20]

Consider making a phone call as an instance. The only thing the individual understands is that inputting the digits and pressing the dial button will result in a phone call; they are unaware of the phone's integrated process or the dial button. That is what we mean by abstraction.

Another real-world example of abstraction is that as television viewers, we can turn it on and off, change the station, and adjust the volume without knowing how the functionality is performed.

Here is how Ruby handles abstraction:

1. **Data Abstraction in Modules:** Modules in Ruby are defined as a collection of methods, classes, and constants. Take the sqrt() function found in the Math module. We just use the sqrt() function in the Math module and pass the number as a parameter whenever we need to calculate the square root of a non-negative integer, without comprehending the exact technique that calculates the square root of the numbers.[21]

2. **Data Abstraction in Classes:** In Ruby, we can accomplish data abstraction using classes. Using access specifiers, we may organize information and methods in the class (private, protected, and public). The class will decide which information should and should not be displayed.

3. **Access Control for Data Abstraction:** Ruby has three layers of access control (private, protected, and public). These are the most essential data abstraction implementations in Ruby. As an instance,

   - Members of a class who have been declared public can be accessed from anywhere in the code.

   - Private members of a class can only be accessible from within the class. They are not allowed to use any script outside of the class.

```ruby
# program to demonstrate the Data Abstraction

class Peeks

    # define publicMethod

    public

    def publicMethod
        puts "In Public"
        # calling privateMethod inside the
publicMethod
        privateMethod
    end

    # define privateMethod

    private

    def privateMethod
        puts "In Private"
    end
end

# create an object of class Peeks
obj = Peeks.new

# call the public method of class Peeks
obj.publicMethod
```

We are not permitted to directly access the privateMethod() of the Peeks class in the aforementioned application; instead, we can call the class's publicMethod() to access the privateMethod().

Advantages of Data Abstraction

- Improves system security by making only critical facts exposed to the user.

- It improves code reusability and reduces code duplication.

- Could change the internal class implementation without impacting the user.

STATIC MEMBERS IN RUBY

Static keywords are mostly used in programming to control memory. The static keyword is used to share a class's identical method or variable across all of its objects. In Ruby, there are various members of a class. When an object is created in Ruby, its methods and variables are included within the object of that class. Methods can be public, private, or protected, but there is no such thing in Ruby as a static method or variable. Ruby lacks a static keyword that indicates that a method belongs to the class level.[22]

Furthermore, a static variable in ruby may be implemented using a class variable, and a static method in ruby can be written using a class variable in one of that class's methods. The static keyword has two implementations in Ruby: variable that is constant and variables in a Class can share by all instances of the class. These variables are known as static variables. Ruby uses a class variable to implement a static variable. When a variable is declared static, space is reserved for it for the duration of the program. The name of the class variable is always preceded by the @@ sign.[23]

Example:

```
# program to demonstrate the Static Variable

class Peeks

    # class variable
    @@peek_count = 0

    def initialize
        @@peek_count += 1
        puts "Number of Peeks = #{@@peek_count}"
    end
end

# create objects of class Peeks
p1 = Peeks.new
p2 = Peeks.new
p3 = Peeks.new
p4 = Peeks.new
```

The Peeks class in the above example has a class variable peek_count. This peek_count property can be shared by all Peeks class instances.

The objects share the static variables. Static method: A static method is one that is shared by all instances of the class. These are known as static methods. In Ruby, static methods may be achieved by utilizing class variables in the class's methods.

Example:

```
# program to demonstrate the Static Method

class Peeks

    #class method
    @@peek_count = 0

    # define instance method
    def incrementPeek
        @@peek_count += 1
    end
    # define class method
    def self.getCount
        return @@peek_count
    end
end

# create objects of class Peeks
g1 = Peeks.new
# call instance method
p1.incrementPeek()

p2 = Peeks.new
# calling instance method
p2.incrementPeek()

p3 = Peeks.new
# calling instance method
p3.incrementPeek()

p4 = Peeks.new
# calling instance method
p4.incrementPeek()

# call class method
puts "Total Number of Peeks = #{Peeks.getCount()}"
```

In the above code, incrementPeek() is a static (class) method of the class Peeks that may be shared by all objects of the class Peeks. Static member functions are only permitted to access static data members or other static member functions; they are not permitted to access nonstatic data members or member functions.

In this chapter, we covered classes and objects, ruby private classes, freezing objects, inheritance and encapsulation, polymorphism, and constructors. Moreover, we discussed access control, mixins, instance variables, data abstraction, and static members in Ruby.

NOTES

1. Object-oriented programming in Ruby | Set 1: https://www.geeksforgeeks. org/object-oriented-programming-in-ruby-set-1/, accessed on August 20, 2022.
2. Object-oriented programming in Ruby | Set 2: https://www.geeksforgeeks. org/object-oriented-programming-in-ruby-set-2/, accessed on August 20, 2022.
3. Ruby | Class and object: https://www.geeksforgeeks.org/ruby-class-object/, accessed on August 22, 2022.
4. Ruby – Classes and objects: https://www.tutorialspoint.com/ruby/ruby_ classes.htm, accessed on August 22, 2022.
5. Private classes in Ruby: https://www.geeksforgeeks.org/private-classes-in-ruby/, accessed on August 22, 2022.
6. Freezing objects | Ruby: https://www.geeksforgeeks.org/freezing-objects-ruby/, accessed on August 22, 2022.
7. How to freeze objects in Ruby?: https://www.tutorialspoint.com/how-to-freeze-objects-in-ruby, accessed on August 22, 2022.
8. Ruby | Inheritance: https://www.geeksforgeeks.org/ruby-inheritance/, accessed on August 22, 2022.
9. Basic of inheritance in Ruby: https://medium.com/@satriajanaka09/basic-of-inheritance-in-ruby-43c8a4fd6b2c, accessed on August 22, 2022.
10. Polymorphism in Ruby: https://www.geeksforgeeks.org/polymorphism-in-ruby/, accessed on August 22, 2022.
11. Ruby | Constructors: https://www.geeksforgeeks.org/ruby-constructors/, accessed on August 22, 2022.
12. Ruby constructors: https://www.includehelp.com/ruby/constructors.aspx, accessed on August 22, 2022.
13. Ruby | Access control: https://www.geeksforgeeks.org/ruby-access-control/, accessed on August 22, 2022.
14. Private methods: http://ruby-for-beginners.rubymonstas.org/advanced/private_methods.html, accessed on August 22, 2022.
15. Ruby | Encapsulation: https://www.geeksforgeeks.org/ruby-encapsulation/, accessed on August 23, 2022.

16. How Does encapsulation work in Ruby?: https://www.tutorialspoint.com/how-does-encapsulation-work-in-ruby, accessed on August 23, 2022.

17. Ruby – Modules and mixins: https://www.tutorialspoint.com/ruby/ruby_modules.htm, accessed on August 23, 2022.

18. Ruby mixins: https://www.geeksforgeeks.org/ruby-mixins/, accessed on August 23, 2022.

19. Instance variables in Ruby: https://www.geeksforgeeks.org/instance-variables-in-ruby/, accessed on August 23, 2022.

20. How to implement data abstraction in Ruby?: https://www.tutorialspoint.com/how-to-implement-data-abstraction-in-ruby, accessed on August 23, 2022.

21. Data abstraction in Ruby: https://www.geeksforgeeks.org/data-abstraction-in-ruby/, accessed on August 23, 2022.

22. Ruby static members: https://www.geeksforgeeks.org/ruby-static-members/, accessed on August 23, 2022.

23. Static members in Ruby programming: https://www.tutorialspoint.com/static-members-in-ruby-programming, accessed on August 23, 2022.

## CHAPTER 3

Basics of Ruby

IN THIS CHAPTER

- ➤ Keywords
- ➤ Data Types
- ➤ Basic Syntax
- ➤ Hello World in Ruby
- ➤ Types of Variables
- ➤ Global Variable in Ruby
- ➤ Comments in Ruby
- ➤ Ranges and Literals
- ➤ Directories
- ➤ Operators
- ➤ Operator Precedence and Overloading in Ruby

In the previous chapter, we covered OOP's concepts in Ruby, and in this chapter, we will discuss the basics of Ruby.

KEYWORDS IN RUBY

Keywords, often known as reserved words, are terms in a language that are used for internal processes or to indicate preset activities. As a result, these

DOI: 10.1201/9781003358510-3

terms may not be used as variable names, objects, or constants.[1] This may cause a compile-time bug.

Example:

```
# program to illustrate Keywords

#!/usr/bin/ruby
# here 'if' is a keyword
# it can't use as variable
if = 22

# 'if' and 'end' are keywords here.
# if condition to check whether
# our age is enough for the voting
if if >= 19
puts "We are eligible to vote."
end
```

Compile Time Error:

```
Error(s), warning(s):

source_file.rb:6: syntax error, unexpected '='
if = 22
  ^

source_file.rb:11: syntax error, unexpected >=
if if >= 19
     ^

source_file.rb:13: syntax error, unexpected keyword_
end, expecting end-of-input
```

Ruby has a total of 41 keywords, as listed below:

Keyword	Description
__ENCODING__	The current file's script encoding.
__LINE__	This keyword's line number in the current file.
__FILE__	The current file's path.
BEGIN	This code executes before any other code in the current file.
END	This code is executed after any other code in the current file.

(Continued)

Keyword	Description
alias	This method creates an alias between two methods (and other things).
and	Short-circuit Boolean expression with lower precedence than &&.
begin	This method begins an exception-handling block.
break	Departs a block early.
case	Begin a case expression.
class	Opens or creates a class.
def	A method is defined.
defined?	Returns a string that describes the argument.
do	Begin a block.
else	In case, if, and unless expressions, the unhandled condition.
elsif	An alternative condition for an if statement.
end	The conclusion of a syntactic block. Classes, modules, methods, exception handling, and control expressions all make use of it.
ensure	Begin a portion of code that is always executed when an exception is thrown.
false	False Boolean
for	A loop comparable to the use of the each method.
if	If and modifier if expressions are supported.
in	In a for loop, this is used to divide the iterable object from the iterator variable.
module	Opens or creates a module.
next	The rest of the block is skipped.
nil	A false value often denotes "no value" or "unknown."
not	The following Boolean expression is inverted. Has less precedence than! Boolean or less precedence than ‖.
or	Execution in the current block is resumed.
redo	Begin a new block.
rescue	In a begin block, begins an exception section of code.
retry	An exception block is retried.
return	A method is exited.
self	The object to which the current method is associated.
super	This method invokes the current function in a superclass.
then	In control structures, this indicates the end of conditional blocks.
true	True Boolean
undef	A class or module is prevented from responding to a method call.
unless	Unless and modifier unless expressions are supported.
until	Creates a loop that will run until the condition is met.
when	A case expression condition.
while	Creates a loop that runs until the condition is met.
yield	Begin the execution of the block passed to the current method.

Example:

```ruby
# program to illustrate use of Keywords

#!/usr/bin/ruby

# define class Vehicle
# using 'class' keyword
class PFP

# define method
# using the 'def' keyword
def peeks

    # print result
    puts "Hello Peeks"

# end of method
# using the 'end' keyword
end

# end of class PFP
# using the 'end' keyword
end

# create object
obj = PFP.new

# call method using object
obj.peeks
```

DATA TYPES IN RUBY

Ruby data types represent many sorts of data such as text, string, integers, and so on. Because it is an object-oriented language, all data types are based on classes.[2] Ruby has several data types, which are as described in the following:

- Numbers
- Boolean
- Strings

- Hashes

- Arrays

- Symbols

Numbers

A number is generally described as a series of digits separated by a dot as a decimal mark. The underscore can use as a separator if desired.[3] There are several types of numbers, such as integers and floats. Ruby is capable of working with both integers and floating point numbers. Integers are classified into two categories based on their size: Bignum and Fixnum.

Example:

```
# program to illustrate
# the Numbers Data Type

# float type
distance = 0.2

# both integer and float type
time = 7.97 / 3900
speed = distance / time
puts "Average speed of sprinter is #{speed} km/h"
```

Boolean

Boolean data types represent simply one piece of data: true or false.

Example:

```
# program to illustrate the
# Boolean Data Type

if true
puts "It is True"
else
puts "It is False"
end

if nil
puts "nil is True"
```

```
else
puts "nil is False"
end

if 0
puts "0 is True"
else
puts "0 is False"
end
```

Strings

A string is a collection of letters that represents a phrase or word. Strings are created by surrounding text in single (') or double ("") quotations. Strings can be created with both double and single quotations. Strings are objects of the String class. Double-quoted strings support substitution and backslash notation, but single-quoted strings do not support substitution and only support backslash notation for \\ and \'.

Example:

```
# program to illustrate
# the Strings Data Type

#!/usr/bin/ruby -w
puts "String Data Type";
puts 'escape using the "\\"';
puts 'That\'s right';
```

Hashes

A hash associates its values with its key. The => symbol assigns a value to a key. A comma separates each key pair, and all of the pairings are surrounded by curly braces. In Ruby, a hash is analogous to an object literal in JavaScript or an associative array in PHP. They are created in the same way as arrays are. A comma at the end is disregarded.

Example:

```
# program to illustrate
# the Hashes Data Type

#!/usr/bin/ruby
```

```ruby
hsh = colors = { "green" => 0x0f0, "blue" =>
0x00f, "red" => 0xf00 }
hsh.each do |key, value|
print key, " is ", value, "\n"
end
```

Arrays

An array is a collection of data or a list of data. It can hold any form of data. Data in an array are separated by commas and contained between square brackets. An array's element positions begin with 0. A comma at the end is disregarded.

Example:

```ruby
# program to illustrate
# the Arrays Data Type

#!/usr/bin/ruby
ary = [ "fred", 12, 3.24, "This is string", "last
element", ]
ary.each do |x|
puts x
end
```

Symbols

Symbols are simple strings. A colon comes before a symbol (:). They are used in place of strings since they take up far less memory. Symbols outperform other data types.

Example:

```ruby
program to illustrate
# the Symbols Data Type

#!/usr/bin/ruby
domains = {:sk => "PeeksforPeeks", :no => "PFP",
:hu => "Peeks"}

puts domains[:sk]
puts domains[:no]
puts domains[:hu]
```

BASIC SYNTAX IN RUBY

Ruby is a purely object-oriented language created in Japan in the mid-1990s by Yukihiro Matsumoto (commonly known as Matz in the Ruby community). Because Ruby's syntax is similar to those of other commonly used languages, it is simple to learn. In this section, we will cover the fundamental syntax of the Ruby programming language.[4]

Let's make a basic code that displays "Hello Everyone."

```
# this line will display "Hello Everyone" as output.
puts "Hello Everyone";
```

End of a Line in Ruby

Ruby considers newline characters (\n) and semicolons (;) to indicate the end of a sentence.

Note: If a line ends with a +, −, or backslash, it denotes the continuation of a sentence.

Whitespace in Ruby

Spaces and tabs are normally disregarded in Ruby code, unless they are in a string, in which case it ignores all spaces in a sentence. However, whitespaces are sometimes employed to evaluate confusing expressions.

Example:

```
m / n interprets as m/n (Here m is a variable)
m n interprets as m(n)
(Here m is a method)

# declaring the function named 'm' which accepts an
# integer and return 1
def m(u) return 1 end

# driver code
m = 3
n = 3

# this m + n interprets as m + n, so prints 6 as output
puts(m + n)
```

```
# this m n interprets as m(n) thus the returned
# value is printed
puts(m n)
```

BEGIN and END Statement in Ruby

The BEGIN statement is used to specify a section of code that must be executed before the program will begin.

Syntax:

```
BEGIN
{
    # code written
}
```

Similarly, END is used to specify a section of code that must be executed at the end of the code.

Syntax:

```
END
{
    # code written
}
```

Example:

```
# program of BEGIN and END
puts "This is the main body of program"

END
{
puts "END of program"
}
BEGIN
{
puts "BEGINNING of Program"
}
```

Comments in Ruby

A comment conceals a section of code from the Ruby Interpreter. Comments can be written in a variety of ways, using the hash symbol (#) at the beginning of each line.

Syntax:

```
#This is the single line comment

#This is the multiple
#lines of comment
=begin
This is another
way of the writing
comments in the
block fashion
=end
```

Identifiers in Ruby

- Variable, constant, and function/method names are examples of identifiers.

- Case sensitive when it comes to Ruby identifiers.[5]

- Ruby identifiers can include alphanumeric letters as well as underscore ( ).

Identifiers include things like Men_1, items_01.

Keywords in Ruby

Ruby keywords are reserved terms in Ruby that can't be used as constant or variable names.

BEGIN	do	next	true
END	else	nil	then
alias	elsif	not	undef
begin	ensure	or	unless
and	end	redo	until
case	for	retry	when
break	false	rescue	while
def	if	self	__FILE__
class	in	return	while

HELLO WORLD IN RUBY

Ruby is a general-purpose computer program that is dynamic, reflective, and object-oriented. Hello World is the simplest basic and first program we create while learning a new programming language. This just prints the phrase "Hello World" on the display. The code to write "Hello world" is shown below.[6]

How May a Ruby Program Execute on a Different System?

We have several platforms on which we can run Ruby programs, which we will go over below:

Using Online IDE

```
puts "Hello World"
```

The code above will execute in an online IDE. The puts keyword is used to display everything on the screen in this case.

With Linux

Using the Command Line To begin, launch a text editor such as Notepad or Notepad++. Create the code in a text editor and save it with the (.rb) extension. Launch the command prompt and proceed through the steps on our device.

To execute the helloworld.rb Ruby script, type ruby helloworld.rb, and the result will be printed.

With Window

Using the Command Line To, see the Ruby version, type ruby -v in the command line window.

To launch the IRB prompt, open our command-line and type irb. After that, we may write the Ruby code, which will be executed through command line.

TYPES OF VARIABLES IN RUBY

In Ruby, there are several sorts of variables:

- Local variables
- Instance variables
- Class variables
- Global variables

Each variable in Ruby is specified by including a special character at the beginning of the variable name, as shown in the table below:[7]

Symbol	Type of variable
[a-z] or _	Local variable
@	Instance variable
@@	Class variable
$	Global variable

Local Variables

A local variable's name must begin with a lowercase letter (a–z) or an underscore (_). These variables are only available in the program construct where they are declared. A local variable is only available within the initialization block. Outside of the procedure, local variables are not accessible. It is not necessary to initialize the local variables.[8]

Example:

```
age = 20
_Age = 30
```

Instance Variables

The name of an instance variable always begins with a @ symbol. They are similar to Class variables in that their values are unique to each instance of an object. Instance variables are accessible across methods for any defined instance or object, implying that instance variables might vary from object to object. It is not necessary to initialize the instance variables, because uninitialized instance variables always have a value of nil.

Example:

```
#!/usr/bin/ruby
# program to illustrate the
# Instance Variables

class Customers

def initialize(id, name, addrs)

# Instance Variables
@cust_id = id
```

```
@cust_name = name
@cust_addrs = addrs
end

# display result
def display_details()
puts "Customers id #@cust_id"
puts "Customers name #@cust_name"
puts "Customers address #@cust_addrs"
end
end

# Create Objects
cust1 = Customers.new("1", "Rohan", "Wisdom
Colony, Amritsar")
cust2 = Customers.new("2", "Payal", "Empire road,
Lucknow")

# Call Methods
cust1.display_details()
cust2.display_details()
```

Class Variables

The name of a class variable always begins with the @@ symbol. It is available across a variety of things. A class variable is a class characteristic that belongs to the class. They must be initialized before being used. Class variables can also be thought of as global variables within the context of a particular class. A class variable is shared by all of the class's descendants. An error will occur if a class variable is not initialized.

Example:

```
#!/usr/bin/ruby
# program to illustrate
# Class Variables

class Customers

# class variable
@@no_of_customers = 0

def initialize(id, name, addrs)
```

```
# instance Variable
@cust_id = id
@cust_name = name
@cust_addrs = addrs
end

# display result
def display_details()
puts "Customers id #@cust_id"
puts "Customers name #@cust_name"
puts "Customers address #@cust_addrs"
end

def total_no_of_customers()

# class variable
@@no_of_customers += 1
puts "Total number of the customers: #@@
no_of_customers"
    end
end

# Create Objects
cust1 = Customers.new("1", "Rohan", "Wisdom
Colony, Delhi")
cust2 = Customers.new("2", "Parul", "Empire road,
Khanna")

# Call Methods
cust1.display_details()
cust1.total_no_of_customers()
cust2.display_details()
cust2.total_no_of_customers()
```

Global Variables

The name of a global variable always begins with $. Class variables cannot be shared between classes. We must define a global variable if we want a single variable that is accessible across classes. It has a global scope, which implies that it may be accessed from anywhere in a program. Uninitialized global variables have a nil value by default, and their use can lead to cryptic and complex scripts.

Example:

```
#!/usr/bin/ruby
# program to illustrate the
# Global Variables

#!/usr/bin/ruby

# global variable
$global_variable = 20
class Class_1
def print_global
puts "Global variable in Class_1 is
#$global_variable"
end
end
class Class_2
def print_global
puts "Global variable in Class_2 is
#$global_variable"
end
end
class_1obj = Class_1.new
class_1obj.print_global
class_2obj = Class_2.new
class_2obj.print_global
```

GLOBAL VARIABLE IN RUBY

Global variable is a global variable that may be accessed from any part of the application. Assigning to global variables from anywhere in the code has global consequences. A dollar symbol ($) is always prefixed to global variables.[9] To have a single variable that is usable across classes, we must define a global variable. An uninitialized global variable has a nil value by default, and its use can lead programs to be cryptic and difficult. Anywhere in the program, a global variable can be changed.

Syntax:

```
$global_variable = 7
```

Example:

```
# Program to understand the Global Variable

# global variable
$global_variable = 20

# Defining class
class Class_1
def print_global
puts "Global variable in the Class_1 is
#$global_variable"
end
end

# Define Another Class
class Class_2
def print_global
puts "Global variable in the Class_2 is
#$global_variable"
end
end

# Create object
class_1obj = Class_1.new
class_1obj.print_global

# Creating another object
class2obj = Class_2.new
class_2obj.print_global
```

In the above code, a global variable with the value 20 is defined. This global variable is accessible from anywhere in the code.

Example:

```
# Program to understand the global variable
$global_variable1 = "PFP"

# Define Class
class Author
def instance_method
```

```
    puts "global vars can use everywhere. See?
#{$global_variable1}, #{$another_global_var}"
end
def self.class_method
    $another_global_var = "Welcome to
PeeksForPeeks"
    puts "global vars can use everywhere. See?
#{$global_variable1}"
end
end

Author.class_method
# "global vars can use everywhere. See? PFP"
# => "global vars can use everywhere. See? PFP"

Author = Author.new
Author.instance_method
# "global vars can use everywhere. See?
# PFP, Welcome to PeeksForPeeks"
# => "global vars can use everywhere. See?
# PFP, Welcome to PeeksForPeeks"
```

In the preceding code, we defined two global variables in a class. We build an Author object and then run the function.

COMMENTS IN RUBY

Comments are statements that are not implemented by the compiler or interpreter. The usage of comments when development makes maintenance and bug detection easier.[10]

There are two kinds of comments in Ruby:

- Single-line comments

- Multiline comments

Here, we will describe both sorts of comments using syntax and examples:

Single-Line Comments

It is symbolized by the # symbol. In Ruby, it is used to express a one-line comment. It's the simplest written comments.[11] When we just require one line of remark in Ruby, we may use the letters "#" before the comment.

Example:

```
# program to show single-line comments

#!/usr/bin/ruby -w

# This is single-line comment.
puts "Single-line comment above"
```

Multiline Comments

If our comment spans more than one line, we may utilize a multiline comment. In Ruby, a multiline comment begins with =begin and ends with =end syntax.

Syntax:

```
=begin
continue
continue
 .
 .
 .
 .
Comment ends
=end
```

Example:

```
# program to show multi-line comments
#!/usr/bin/ruby -w

puts "Multi-line comments below"

=begin
Comment line-1
Comment line-2
Comment line-3
=end
```

RANGES IN RUBY

Ruby ranges represent a set of values with a start and an end point. A range's values can be integers, characters, strings, or objects.[12] It is built with start_point...end_point, start_point...end_point literals, or with::new. It adds flexibility to the program while also reducing its size.

Example:

```
# program to demonstrate the
# Range in Ruby

# Array value separator
$, =", "

# using the start_point..end_point
# to_a is used to convert
# it into array
range_op = (5. . 12).to_a

# display result
puts "#{range_op}"

# using start_point...end_point
# to_a is used to convert
# it into array
range_op1 = (5 ... 12).to_a

# display result
puts "#{range_op1}"
```

Ruby offers three different forms of ranges:

- Ranges as sequences

- Conditions as ranges

- Intervals as ranges

Ranges as Sequences

This is a common and straightforward approach to construct Ruby ranges to produce subsequent values in the series.[13] It has a start and an end point. For constructing ranges, two operators are used: the double dot (..) operator and the triple dot (...) operator.

Example:

```
# program to illustrate ranges as sequences

#!/usr/bin/ruby

# input value which lies between the
# range 5 and 9
ranges = 5..9

# print true if value is lies
# between range otherwise
# print false
puts ranges.include?(3)

# print maximum value which lies
# between the range
ans = ranges.max
puts "Maximum value = #{ans}"

# print minimum value which lies
# between the range
ans = ranges.min
puts "Minimum value = #{ans}"


# Iterate 3 times from 5 to 9
# and print the value
ranges.each do |digit|
puts "In Loop #{digit}"
end
```

Ranges as Conditions

In looping, ranges may also be expressed as conditional expressions. Conditions are included inside the start and end statements in this case.

Example:

```
# program to illustrate ranges as condition

#!/usr/bin/ruby

# given number
num = 5132
```

```
result = case num
when 2000..3000 then "Lies Between 2000 and 3000"
when 3000..4000 then "Lies Between 3000 and 4000"
when 5000..6000 then "Lies Between 5000 and 6000"
when 7000..8000 then "Lies Between 7000 and 8000"

else "Above 8000"
end

puts result
```

Ranges as Intervals

Ranges can also specify in terms of intervals to determine whether or not a particular value falls inside the range. The equality operator (===) is used to express it.

Example:

```
# program to illustrate ranges as intervals

#!/usr/bin/ruby

# using if statement
if (('A'..'Z') === 'E')

# display the value
puts "E lies in the range of A to Z"

# end of if
end

# using if statement
if ((1..100) === 66)

# display the value
puts "66 lies in the range of 1 to 100"

# end of if
end
```

If we try to utilize the reverse range operator in Ruby, nothing will be returned because range operators yield nothing if the right side value is less than the left side value. Always use the reverse() function with range operators to output the reverse order of a specified range.

```
# program to print the reverse
# order using range operator

#!/usr/bin/ruby

# using the ranges but
# it will not give any output
puts ('Z'..'U').to_a

# using the reverse() method which will
# print given range in reverse order
  puts ('U'..'Z').to_a.reverse
```

LITERALS IN RUBY

A literal/constant is any constant value that may be allocated to a variable. When typing an object in Ruby code, we always use literal.[14] Ruby Literals are similar to those of other computer languages, with a few changes and peculiarities.

Ruby literals are as follows:

- Booleans and nil

- Numbers or Integers

- Ranges

- Strings

- Symbols

- Arrays

- Hashes

- Regular expressions

Booleans and Nil

The Boolean constants are as follows. In this case, false and nil behave similarly, despite the fact that nil denotes unknown or empty.[15] It works similarly as false in conditional statements, except it only returns true or false constants. A positive variable is true act the same.

```
true, false, nil
```

Example:

```
# Demo for the Boolean literals
puts(4+6==10);# returns true
puts(4+6!=10);# returns false
puts(4+6==nil);# return false
```

Numbers or Integers

Ruby handles all Integer types. Integers of any size can be written as 200, 2_00, or 20_0. Ruby permits any amount of '_' in its numerals for readability reasons.

Syntax:

```
decimal(0d or 0D)
octal(0o or 0O or 0)
hex-decimal(0x or 0X)
binary(0b or 0B).
float(num- or numE1)
```

Example:

```
puts("400+1_00+10_0=", 400+1_00+10_0 );
puts("hexa-", 0xaa );
puts("octal-", 0o333 );
puts("decimal-", 0d180, " ", 180);
puts("binary-", 0b1010);
puts("Float-", 1.335E1);
puts("hexa-", aa);# error
```

String

It's the same as Python. The string can be stated using "" or "," where "" allows for interpolation of escaped characters.

Syntax:

```
#{expression}
```

Example:

```
puts( "Three multiply four is Twelve : #{3 * 4}")
puts("guardians\nof\nthe\ngalaxy");
puts('guardians\nof\nthe\ngalaxy')
```

Symbol

A symbol in Ruby indicates a name within the interpreter. Symbols are never garbage-collected and are always placed inside the Ruby interpreter. As a result, if a large number of interpreters are generated or never released, the size of the interpreter is affected.

Syntax:

```
ruby_symbol
```

Interpolation can also be used to generate symbol keys:

```
puts(:":guardian_id#{30+2_5}")
```

Ranges

It's comparable to the one in the Python range (). Displays all possible values between the limits specified (including).

Syntax:

```
range1..range2
```

Example:

```
for x in 2..5 do
    puts(x)
end
```

Array

Arrays are collections of things generated with the "[" and "]" operators.

Example:

```
# Code for the Array Demo
gog = ['Quill', 'Gamora', 'Rocket', 'Groot',
'Drax']
puts(gog[0])
puts(gog[2])

# Negative indices are counted from end
print("The Negative Index:", gog[-4], "\n\n")
```

```
# [start, count]
puts("[start, count]:", gog[0, 4], "\n")

# Using the ranges.
# as range size exceeded it prints till full
length
puts("Using the range:", gog[0..8])
```

Hashes

It's comparable to the one in Python. We may generate a hash using symbol keys since they are unchangeable once formed and can be used as ideal keys.

Syntax:

```
{key:value}
```

Example:

```
# way of create hash
hash1 = Hash.new

# way of create hash
hash2 = {}

# initialize values and keys
hash1 = {"Quill" => 200, "Drax" => 400, "Gamora"
=> 600}

# initialize values and keys with symbol keys
hash2 = {Quill:1, Gamora:2}
print(hash1.keys, "\n")
print(hash2.keys, "\n")
for x in hash2.keys do

# : Should use while checking before
# its a part of the symbol key
    if x==:Quill

    # Printing value and assigned key
        print(x, "=>", hash2[x], "\n")
    end
end
```

Regular Expression

It is comparable to the one found in Perl {/pattern/}. Ruby Regexps can define with or without delimiters.

Syntax:

```
/pattern/ or %r{pattern}
```

We may generate a hash utilizing symbol keys since they are unchangeable once formed and serve as the perfect key.

Syntax:

```
{key:value}
```

Example:

```
line1 = "guardians of galaxy";
line2 = "Doctor Strange";

# Checks whether 'of' is in line1 in the // format
if ( line1 =~ /of(.*)/ )
puts line1
end

# Checks whether 'Doc' is in line1 in the %r{}
format.
if ( line2 =~ %r{Doc(.*)} )
puts line2
end

# Checks whether 'off' is in the line1.
if ( line2 =~ /off(.*)/ )
puts line2
else
    puts "nothing"
end
```

DIRECTORIES IN RUBY

A directory is a storage space for files. The Dir class and the FileUtils module manage directories in Ruby, whereas the File class manages files.[16]

The parent directory for directories is denoted by a double dot (..), whereas the directory itself is denoted by a single dot (.).

The Dir Class

In Ruby, the Dir class allows access to and the contents of file system directory hierarchies. It allows us to list the contents of folders, generate file names with suitable path separators, and so on.

The Dir class has the following characteristics:

Ruby Directory Creation

To make a directory, use the mkdir() function of the Dir class.[17] To construct a non-nested directory, use the following code; the mkdir() function returns 0 if the directory is successfully formed.

Syntax:

```
Dir.mkdir "name-of-directory"
```

Example:

```
# create directory
f=Dir.mkdir "mno"

# a directory named mno is created
print("#{f}")
```

Examining Ruby Directories

The exists() function of the Dir class is used to determine whether or not a directory exists.

Syntax:

```
Dir.exist?"name-of-directory"
```

Example:

```
# create directory
puts Dir.mkdir("folder")

# checking if directory exists or not
puts Dir.exists?("folder")
```

The empty? function of the Dir class is used to determine whether or not a directory is empty.

Syntax:

```
Dir.empty? "name-of-directory"
```

Example:

```
# create directory
puts Dir.mkdir("folder")

# checking if directory is empty or not
puts Dir.empty?("folder")
```

Working with Ruby Directories

For Ruby directory operations, the Dir class implements several methods such as new(), pwd(), home(), path(), getwd(), chdir(), entries(), glob(), and so on.

- To generate a new directory object, use new().

  Syntax:

  ```
  obj=Dir.new("name-of-directory")
  ```

- The folder directory should already exist in the script above.

- The Dir class's pwd() function returns the current directory.

  Syntax:

  ```
  Dir.pwd
  ```

  Example:

  ```
  # create directory
  Dir.mkdir("folder")

  # returns the current working directory
  puts Dir.pwd
  ```

- The home() function in the Dir class is used to return the current user's home directory.

Syntax:

```
Dir.home
```

Example:

```
# create directory
Dir.mkdir("folder")

# returns the home directory
puts Dir.home
```

- The code below will retrieve a particular user's home directory.

```
Dir.home('username')
```

- The path argument is returned by the Dir class's path() function.

Syntax:

```
dr=Dir.new("name-of-directory")
dr.path
```

Example:

```
# create directory
Dir.mkdir("folder")

# create object of that directory using new()
method
obj=Dir.new("folder")

# assigns path parameter of obj to variable fr
fr=obj.path
print("#{fr}")
```

- The getwd() function of the Dir class is employed to return the current directory path.

Syntax:

```
Dir.getwd
```

Example:

```
# create directory
Dir.mkdir("folder")

# returns path of the current working directory
puts Dir.getwd
```

- The Dir class's chdir() function is used to change the current directory.

Syntax:

```
Dir.chdir("name-of-directory")
```

Example:

```
# create directories
Dir.mkdir("/workspace/folder1")
Dir.mkdir("/workspace/folder2")

# display the path of current directory
puts Dir.pwd

# change the current working directory
Dir.chdir("folder2")
puts Dir.pwd
```

- The entries() function of the Dir class can be used to return an array of all the files and directories contained in the directory.

Syntax:

```
Dir.entries("directory")
```

Example:

```
# create a directory named folder
Dir.mkdir("folder")

# display the path of current directory
puts Dir.pwd
```

```
# change current working directory to folder
Dir.chdir("folder")
puts Dir.pwd

# create directories inside folder
Dir.mkdir("subfolder1")
Dir.mkdir("subfolder2")
Dir.mkdir("subfolder3")

# display all files and folders present in
folder
print("Entries:\n")
puts Dir.entries("C:/Users/KIIT/Desktop/folder")
```

- The glob() function in the Dir class can be used to display all files that match a specific pattern.

Syntax:

```
Dir.glob("pattern")
```

Example:

```
# create a directory named folder
Dir.mkdir("folder")

# change current working directory to folder
Dir.chdir("folder")

# create directories inside folder
Dir.mkdir("pmnoq")
Dir.mkdir("mnop")
Dir.mkdir("program.rb")
Dir.mkdir("program2.rb")

# displaying specified files and folders
print"\nAll files in the current working
directory: \n"
puts Dir.glob("*")
print"\nAll files containing 'abc' in the name: \n"
puts Dir.glob("*mno*")
print"\nAll ruby files: \n"
puts Dir.glob("*.rb")
```

Deleting Ruby Directories

There are several methods in class Dir for removing Ruby Directories, including rmdir(), delete(), and unlink().

Syntax:

```
Dir.delete "folders"
Dir.rmdir "folders"
Dir.unlink "folders"
```

Example:

```
#create directory
Dir.mkdir("folders")
puts Dir.exist?("folders")

# delete directory
Dir.rmdir("folders")
puts Dir.exist?("folders")
```

Constructing Nested Directories

The FileUtils module's mkdir_p() function is used to generate a directory and all of its parent directories.

Syntax:

```
FileUtils.mkdir_p 'directory_path'
```

Example:

```
# create directory parent_folder
Dir.mkdir "parent_folder"
print("The Current Directory: ")
puts Dir.pwd
require "fileutils"

# create nested directory in the parent_folder
FileUtils.mkdir_p "parent_folder/child_folder/
folder"

# change current directory to parent_folder
```

```
Dir.chdir("/workspace/parent_folder")
print("The Current Directory: ")
puts Dir.pwd
# check child folder exists or not
puts Dir.exists?("child_folder")

# change current directory to child_folder
Dir.chdir("/workspace/parent_folder/child_folder")
print("The Current Directory: ")
puts Dir.pwd

# check folder exists or not
puts Dir.exists?("folder")
```

Transferring Files and Folders

The FileUtils module's mv() and move() methods are utilized to move files and folders from the current directory to the target location.

Syntax:

```
FileUtils.mv("source", "destination")
```

Example:

```
# create directories
Dir.mkdir "folders1"
Dir.mkdir "folders2"
require "fileutils"

# moving directory folders1 into directory
folders2
FileUtils.mv( "folders1", "folders2")

# changing current directory to folders2
Dir.chdir("folders2")

# checking if folders1 exists in folders2
puts Dir.exists?("folders1")
```

Transferring Files from One Directory to Another

The FileUtils module's cp() function is utilized to copy files from the current directory to the target directory.

Syntax:

```
FileUtils.cp("source", "destination")
```

Example:

Consider the following two directories: folders1 and folders2, both of which contain the file test1.txt.

```
require "fileutils"

# copying test1.txt from folders1 to folders2
FileUtils.cp( "folders2/test1.txt", "folders1")
Dir.chdir("folders1")

# checking if test1.txt exists in folders1
puts File.exist?("test1.txt")
```

OPERATORS IN RUBY

An operator is a sign that denotes a procedure to be carried out with one or more operands. Operators are the basic components of every computer language. Operators allow us to do numerous actions on operands. Ruby has several types of operators, which are as follows:

Arithmetic Operators

These are used to carry out arithmetic and mathematical functions on operands.

- Addition (+): The addition (+) operator joins two operands. For instance, x + y.

- Subtraction (−): Subtraction of two operands. For instance, x − y.

- Multiplication (×): multiplies two operands. For instance, x × y.

- Division (/): divides the first operand by second operand. For instance, x/y.

- Modulus (%): When the first operand is divided by the second, the modulus (%) operator returns the remainder. For instance, x%y.

- Exponent (**): This operator returns the operands' exponential (power). For instance, x**y.

Example:

```
# program to demonstrate the
# Arithmetic Operators

# Addition
puts ("Addition:")
puts (20 + 30)

# Subtraction
puts ("Subtraction:")
puts (50 - 30)

# Division
puts ("Division:")
puts (200 / 40)

# Multiplication
puts ("Multiplication:")
puts (20 * 30)

# Modulus
puts ("Modulus:")
puts (30 % 6)

# Exponent
puts ("Exponent:")
puts (4 ** 8)
```

Comparison Operators

Comparison operators, also known as relational operators, are used to compare two values. Let's go over them one by one:

- The equal to (==) operator determines whether or not two operands are equal. If this is case, it returns true. If not, it returns false. 6==6 will, for example, return true.

- The not equal to (!=) operator determines whether or not two operands are equal. If it does not, it returns true. If not, it returns false. It is the Boolean equivalent of the "==" operator. 6!=6 will, for example, return false.

- The greater than (>) operator determines if the first operand is greater than the second. If this is case, it returns true. If not, it returns false. 7>6 will, for example, yield true.

- The less than (<) operator determines if the first operand is less than the second. If this is case, it returns true. If not, it returns false. 7<6, for example, will return false.

- The greater than equal to (>=) operator determines if the first and second operands are greater than or equal. If this is case, it returns true. If not, it returns false. 6>=6 will, for example, yield true.

- The operator less than equal to (<=) determines if the first operand is less than or equal to the second operand. If this is the case, it returns true. If not, it returns false. 6=6 will, for example, also yield true.

- The combined combination (<=>) operator returns 0 when the first and second operands are equal, 1 when the first operand is greater than second, and −1 when the first operand is less than the second.

- Operator for case equality (===) It will check for equality in the case statement.

- ".eql?" If the receiver and argument are of the same type and have equal values, this operator returns true.

- "Equal?" This particular operator If the receiver and argument have the same object id, this function returns true.

Example:

```
# program to demonstrate the
# Comparison Operators

puts "Equal To Operator:"
puts (20 == 30)

puts "Not Equal To Operator:"
puts (50 != 30)

puts "Greater than Operator"
puts (120 > 40)
```

```
puts "Less than Operator"
puts (20 < 40)

puts "Less than Equal To Operator"
puts (4 <= 8)

puts "Greater than Equal To Operator"
puts (3 >= 8)

puts "Combined combination operator"
puts (30 <=> 30)
puts (20 <=> 30)
puts (30 <=> 20)
```

Logical Operators

They are used to integrate two or more conditions/constraints or to enhance the assessment of the original condition.[18] These are as follows:

- When both of the conditions in question are met, the logical AND(&&) operator returns true. If not, it returns false. The "and" operator is an alternative to the && operator. a && b, for instance, returns true when both a and b are true (i.e., nonzero).

- When one (or both) of the criteria in question are met, the logical OR(||) operator returns true. If not, it returns false. The "or" operator is an alternative to the || operator. For instance, a || b returns true if either an or b is true (i.e., non-zero). Naturally, it returns true if both a and b are true.

- If the condition is not met, the logical NOT(!) operator returns true. If not, it returns false. The "not" operator is an alternative to the! operator. !true, for instance, returns false.

Example:

```
# program to demonstrate the
# Logical Operators

# Variables
c = 20
d = 40
e = 30
```

```
# using && operator
if c == 20 && d == 40 && e == 30
    puts "Logical AND Operator"
    puts result = c * d * e
end

# using || operator
puts "Logical OR operator"
if c == 40 || d == 40
    puts result = c + d + e
end

# using ! operator
puts "Logical Not Operator"
puts !(true)
```

Assignment Operators

When allocating a value to a variable, assignment operators are employed. The assignment operator's left operand is a variable, while the assignment operator's right operand is a value. Otherwise, compiler will throw an error if value on the right side is not of same data-type as the variable on left side.

The following are examples of assignment operators:

- The simplest assignment operator is the equals symbol (=). This operator is used to assign the variable on the left the value on the right.

- The Add AND Assignment (+=) operator is used to combine the left and right operands and then assign the result to a variable on left.

- The Subtract AND Assignment (−=) operator is used to subtract the left operand from the right operand and then assign result to left operand's variable.

- The Multiply AND Assignment (*=) operator is used to multiply the left operand by the right operand and then assign result to left operand variable.

- The Divide AND Assignment (/=) operator divides the left operand by the right operand and then assigns the result to a variable on left.

- The Modulus AND Assignment (%=) operator is used to assign the modulo of the left operand to the right operand and then to a variable on the left.

- The Exponent AND Assignment (**=) operator is used to increase the power of the left operand and assign it to a variable on left.

Example:

```
# program to demonstrate the
# Assignments Operators

puts "Simple assignment operator"
puts m = 30

puts "Add AND assignment operator"
puts m += 20

puts "Subtract AND assignment operator"
puts m -= 7

puts "Multiply AND assignment operator"
puts m *= 20

puts "Divide AND assignment operator"
puts m /= 6

puts "Modulus AND assignment operator"
puts m %= 2

puts "Exponent AND assignment operator"
puts m **= 4
```

Bitwise Operators

Ruby has six bitwise operators that act at the bit level or are used to conduct bit-by-bit operations.[19] The bitwise operators are as follows:

- Bitwise AND (&) takes two operands and performs AND on each bit of the two numbers. AND returns 1 only if both bits are 1.

- Bitwise OR (|) takes two operands and performs OR on each bit of the two integers. OR yields 1 if any of the two bits is 1.

- Bitwise XOR (^) takes two operands and performs XOR on each bit of the two numbers. If the two bits are different, the result of XOR is 1.

- Shift left (<<) takes two integers, left shifts the bits of the first operand, and the amount of places to shift is determined by the second operand.

- Right shift (>>) takes two integers, right shifts the bits of the first operand, and the number of places to shift is determined by the second operand.

- Complementary (~): This operator accepts a single integer and performs an 8-bit complement operation.

Example:

```
# program to demonstrate the
# Bitwise Operators

# variables
m = 10
n = 20

puts "Bitwise AND operator"
puts (m & n)

puts "Bitwise OR operator"
puts (m |n)

puts "Bitwise XOR operator"
puts (m ^ n)

puts "Bitwise Complement operator"
puts (~m)

puts "Binary right shift operator"
puts (m >> 2)

puts "Binary left shift operator"
puts (m << 2)
```

Ternary Operator

It is a conditional operator, which is a shortcut for the if-else expression. It contains three operands, therefore the term "ternary." Depending on the value of a Boolean expression, it will return one of two results.

Syntax:

```
condition ? first-expression : second-expression;
```

Explanation:

```
condition: It evaluate to true or false.

If condition is true
 first-expression is evaluated and becomes result.

If condition is false,
 second-expression is evaluated and becomes
result.
```

Example:

```
# program to demonstrate the
# Ternary Operator

# variable
Marks-obtained = 100

# using ternary operator
result = marks-obtained > 50?  'Pass' : 'Fail'

# display output
puts result
```

Range Operators

Range operators are used in Ruby to create the given sequence range of defined items. Ruby has two range operators, which are as follows:

- The double dot (..) operator is used to specify a sequence range in which both the beginning and terminating elements are included. For example, 6...9 will generate a sequence that looks like 6, 7, 8, 9.

- The triple dot (...) operator is used to specify a sequence range in which only the first element is inclusive and the last element is exclusive. For example, 6...9 will generate a sequence that looks like 6, 7, 8.

Example:

```
# program to demonstrate the
# Range Operator

# Array value separator
$, =", "

# using. . Operator
range_op = (6. . 9).to_a

# display result
puts "#{range_op}"

# using ... Operator
range_op1 = (6 ... 9).to_a

# display result
puts "#{range_op1}"
```

defined? Operator

defined? operator is a particular operator that determines whether or not the passed expression is defined. If the passed argument is not defined, it returns nil; else, it returns a string containing the definition of that parameter.

Syntax:

```
defined? Expression-to-be-checked
```

Example:

```
# program to demonstrate the
# defined? Operator

# variables
PFP = 1
Peeks = 80
```

```
puts ("define? Operator Results")

# using defined? Operator
# it returns constant
puts defined? PFP

# it returns constant
puts defined? Peeks

# it returns expression
puts defined? a

# it returns expression
puts defined? 60
```

Dot "." and Double Colon "::" Operators

- To access a class's methods, use the dot (.) operator.

- The double colon (::) operator is used to access constants, class methods, and instance methods specified within a class or module from anywhere outside the class or module. The crucial thing to understand is that in Ruby, classes and methods may be regarded constants, and you can also prefix the :: Const name with the expression that yields the right class object. If no prefix expression is specified, the main Object class is utilized by default.

Example:

```
# program to demonstrate
# Dot "." and Double Colon
# "::" Operators

# defined constant on the main Object class
CONS = 7

# define module
module Peeks

CONS = 7

# set global CONS to 9
::CONS = 9
```

```
    # set local CONS to 12
CONS = 12
end

# displaying global CONS value
puts CONS

# displaying local "Peeks" CONS value
# using :: operator
puts Peeks::CONS

class Pfp
    def Peeks2
        puts "Dot Operator"
    end
end

# calling Peeks2 module using
# Dot(.) operator
puts Pfp.new.Peeks2
```

OPERATOR PRECEDENCE IN RUBY

Operators are employed to perform various operations on operands. Operator precedence determines which operator is performed first in an expression having several operators with differing precedence.[20] Associativity is utilized when two operators with the same precedence exist in an expression. Because "*" and "/" have the same precedence, the equation "200/20 * 20" is written as "(200/20) * 20."

```
20 + 40 * 10 is calculated as 20 + (40 * 10)
and not as (20 + 40) * 10
```

The following table illustrates operators with the highest precedence at the top and operators with the lowest precedence at the bottom.

Operator	Category
[ ] [ ]=	Element reference, element set
**	Exponentiation
!, ~, +	Boolean NOT, bitwise complement, unary plus
*, /, %	Multiplication, division, modulo (remainder)

(Continued)

Operator	Category
+, −	Addition (or concatenation), subtraction
< <, > >	Bitwise shift-left (or append), bitwise shift-right
&	Bitwise AND
|, ^	Bitwise OR, bitwise XOR
>, >=, <, <=	Ordering
<=>, ==, ===, !=, =~, !~	Equality, pattern matching, comparison
&&	Logical AND
||	Boolean OR
| |	Logical OR
.., ...=	Range creation and Boolean flip-flops
?, :	Conditional
modifier-rescue	Exception-handling modifier
=, +=, −=, etc.	Assignment
defined?	Test variable definition and type
not	Boolean NOT (low precedence)
or, and	Boolean OR, Boolean AND
modifier-if, modifier-unless, modifier-while, modifier-until	Conditional and loop modifiers
begin/end	Blocks

Example:

```
# program to show the Operators Precedence

    m = 30;
    n = 10;
    o = 15;
    p = 5;
    q = 0

# operators with highest precedence
# will operate the first
q = m + n * o / p;

    # step 1: 30 + (10 * 15) /5
    # step 2: 30 + (150 /5)
    # step 3:(30 + 30)

puts"Value of m + n * o / p is : #{q}"
```

OPERATOR OVERLOADING IN RUBY

Ruby has operator overloading, which allows us to specify how an opera-tor should be used in a certain program. The a "+" operator, for instance, can be defined to do subtraction rather than addition, and vice versa. Overloaded operators include +, -, /, *, **, %, and so on, whereas operators that cannot be overloaded include &, &&, |, ||, (), {}, ~, and so on. Normal functions and operator functions are the same.[21] The main distinction is that the name of an operator function is always accompanied by a symbol of the operator. When the corresponding operator is employed, the opera-tor functions are called. Because operator overloading is not commutative, 3 + a is not the same as a + 3. When 3 + a is attempted, it will fail. The fol-lowing example is an illustration of Ruby operator overloading.

```
# program of the Operator Overloading
class Cars
      attr_accessor:name, :color

      # Initialize name and color
      def initialize(name, color)
            @name = name
            @color = color
      end
      def +(obj)
            return Cars.new("#{self.name}#{obj.name}",
                    "#{self.color}#{obj.color}")
      end
end
m = Cars.new("BMW", "Black")
n = Cars.new("Audi", "White")
puts (m+n).inspect
```

As we see, the "+" operator has been overloaded, and so it returns the two concatenated string outputs of name and color. This is yet another instance using the same program, but instead of the "+" operator, we have overloaded the "/" operator.

Example:

```
# program of Operator Overloading
class Cars
      attr_accessor:name, :color
```

```
    # Initialize name and color
    def initialize(name, color)
        @name = name
        @color = color
    end
    def /(obj)
        return Cars.new("#{self.name}#{obj.name}",
                        "#{self.color}#{obj.color}")
    end
end
c = Cars.new("BMW", "Black")
d = Cars.new("Audi", "Red")
puts (c/d).inspect
```

We observe that the result is the same since we have overloaded the "/" operator to execute concatenation in the preceding instance; hence, we may overload any operator regardless of its typical usage.[22] We will try to overload analogous operators in the following instance (note: we'll be using the Ruby module Comparable for this). The Comparable module in Ruby is used by the class whose objects may be ordered. It returns −1 if the receiver is less than another object, and 0 if the receiver is equal to another object. It returns 1 if the receiver is greater than another object.

Example:

```
# program of the Operator Overloading
class Comparable-operator
    include Comparable
    attr_accessor:name

    # Initialize name
    def initialize(name)
        @name=name
    end
    def <=>(obj)
        return self.name<=>obj.name
    end
end
c = Comparable-operator.new("Peeks for Peeks")
d = Comparable-operator.new("Operator
Overloading")
puts c<=>d
```

PREDEFINE VARIABLES AND CONSTANTS IN RUBY

We will discuss predefine variables and constants here.

Predefine Variables in Ruby

Ruby comes with a plethora of predefined variables. Each preset variable has its own set of rules. Predefine variables can be used to do a single job, such as when working with interpreter arguments or regular expressions. The following is a list of predefined variables in Ruby:

Variables	Description
$!	It stores an exception information message that was set by the previous "raise." The Alias of $ERROR_INFO.
$@	It contains an array containing the backtrace of the most recent exception generated. The Alias of $ERROR_POSITION.
$/	The input record separator, which is usually a newline. If it is set to nil, the entire file is read at once. The Alias of $INPUT_RECORD_SEPARATOR.
$\	The output separator for print and IO#write, which is set to nil by default. The Alias of $OUTPUT_RECORD_SEPARATOR
23$,	The print output field separator and the default separator for Array#join. The Alias of $OUTPUT_FIELD_SEPARATOR.
$;	String#split uses it as the default separator. The Alias of $FIELD_SEPARATOR.
$.	It stores the current input line number from the previous file. The Alias of $INPUT_LINE_NUMBER.
$<	An object that allows access to the concatenation of the contents of all files specified as command line arguments or $stdin. The Alias of $DEFAULT_INPUT.
$>	It is the output destination for kernel.print and kernel.printf, with the default value of $stdout. The Alias of $DEFAULT_OUTPUT.
$&	The string that was matched by the previous pattern match. The Alias of $MATCH.
$'	The string immediately to the left of the last pattern match. The Alias of $PREMATCH.
$'	The string immediately to the right of the last pattern match. The Alias of $POSTMATCH.
$+	The string connected to the last matched group in the previous successful pattern match. The Alias of $LAST_PAREN_MATCH.
$1-$9	The string that matched in the nth group of the last successfully matched pattern.
$_	In the current scope, the last input line read by get or readline. It is a variable that exists only locally. The Alias of $LAST_READ_LINE.

(Continued)

Variables	Description
$~	It contains data about the most recent match in the current scope. It is one of the local variables. The Alias of $LAST_MATCH_INFO.
$-p	If option -p is set, it is true (loop mode is on). The variable is read-only.
$-l	If option -l is set, this is true (line-ending process is on). The variable is read-only.
$-i	If in-place-edit mode is enabled, this variable will contain the extension; otherwise, it will be null.
$-a	If option -a is set, it is true (autosplit mode is one). The variable is read-only.
$-d	Level of -d is switch. The Alias of $DEBUG.
$-v	The verbose flag. The -v switch configures it. The Alias of $VERBOSE.
$-K	The source code's character encoding. The Alias of $KCODE.
$0	It includes the name of the script that is being run.
$$	The process number of the currently running Ruby application. The Alias of $PROCESS_ID.
$?	The last child process's state has changed to terminated. The Alias of $CHILD_STATUS.
$:	Load paths for programs and binary modules that are required or loaded. The Alias of $LOAD_PATH.
$FILENAME	The name of the current input file reads from $<. Same as $<.filename.
$stderr	The Current standard error output.
$stdin	The Current standard input.
$stdout	The Current standard output.
$=	Flag for the case-sensitive, nil by default. The Alias of $IGNORECASE
$*	Command line argument given for program, also known as ARGV. The Alias of ARGV.
$"	The Array contains the module name loaded by require. The Alias of $LOAD_FEATURES.

Example:

```
# program to illustrate
# the use of pre-defined Variables


# Using '$0' To know about
# the script name
puts "Script_name: ",$0;


# Using ' #{$$}' to know about total
# number of the process in the script
puts "The Total number of process in this script:
#{$$}"
```

```
# Using $; as default separator
# for String#split.
m = "6,2,4,8,3,6,7"
$; = ","
p m.split


# Pattern matching
"Welcome to PeeksforPeeks Portal!" =~ /Peeks/

# use to print string to the
# left of last pattern match
p $`

# use to print string matched
# by last pattern match
p $&

# use to print string to the
# right of last pattern match
p $'
```

Predefined Constants in Ruby

Ruby has a large number of predefined constants. The following is a list of predefined constants:

Constant name	Description
TRUE	The Equivalent to true.
FALSE	The Equivalent to false.
NIL	The Equivalent to nil.
STDIN	$stdin's standard input and default value.
STDOUT	$stdout's default value is standard output.
STDERR	Standard output error and $stderr default value.
RUBY_VERSION	A string indicating the Ruby interpreter version.
RUBY_PLATFORM	A string indicating the platform of the Ruby interpreter.
RUBY_RELEASE_DATE	A string indicating the Ruby interpreter's release date.
DATA	The program's file object, pointing right after the __END__. And not defined if __END__ is missing from the code.
ARGV	The command-line arguments given to the program are stored in an array. Alias of $*.
ARGF	A virtual concatenation of files provided as command-line arguments is accessible via this object. Alias of $<.
ENV	It's a hash-like object that holds the current environment variables.

It is advised that we use true, false, and nil since they are backward-compatible.

Example:

```
# program to illustrate
# the pre-defined Constants

# To know about the Ruby Version
d = RUBY_VERSION
puts "The Current Version: #{d}"

# To Know about the Ruby Platform
e = RUBY_PLATFORM
puts "The Platform of Ruby: #{e}"

# To know about the Ruby Release Date
f = RUBY_RELEASE_DATE
puts "The Release date of Ruby: #{f}"
```

THE UNLESS STATEMENT AND UNLESS MODIFIER IN RUBY

Ruby has a specific statement known as the except statement. When the provided condition is false, this statement is performed. It is the inverse of an if statement. The piece of code in the if statement operates once the supplied condition is true, whereas the piece of code in the unless statement executes once the provided condition is false.[24]

We cannot use if statement and or operator to print false statements unless statement is used when we need to display false condition because if statement and or operator usually operates on true condition.

Syntax:

```
unless condition

    # code..

else

    # code..

end
```

Flowchart:

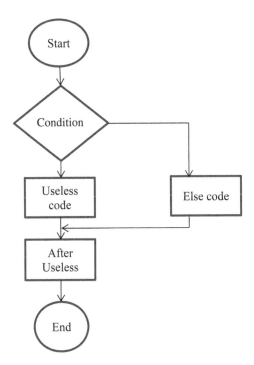

Unless statement in Ruby.

The Unless Modifier

We may also use unless as a modifier to change the meaning of an expression.[25] When we use except as a modifier, the left side becomes a then condition and the right side becomes a test condition.

Syntax:

```
statement unless condition
```

Example:

```
# program to illustrate
# the unless modifier

# variable d
d = 0
```

```
# unless is behave as modifier
# here 'd += 2 ' is statement
# d.zero? is condition
d += 2 unless d.zero?
    puts(d)
```

In this chapter, we covered keywords, data types, basic syntax, hello world program, and types of variables. Moreover, we discussed global variable, comments, ranges and literals, directories, operator precedence, and overloading.

NOTES

1. Ruby | Keywords: https://www.geeksforgeeks.org/ruby-keywords/, accessed on August 23, 2022.
2. Ruby | Data types: https://www.geeksforgeeks.org/ruby-data-types/, accessed on August 23, 2022.
3. Ruby data types: https://www.javatpoint.com/ruby-data-types, accessed on August 23, 2022.
4. Ruby basic syntax: https://www.geeksforgeeks.org/ruby-basic-syntax/, accessed on August 24, 2022.
5. Ruby – syntax: https://www.tutorialspoint.com/ruby/ruby_syntax.htm, accessed on August 24, 2022.
6. Hello world in Ruby: https://www.geeksforgeeks.org/hello-world-in-ruby/, accessed on August 24, 2022.
7. Ruby | Types of variables: https://www.geeksforgeeks.org/ruby-types-of-variables/, accessed on August 24, 2022.
8. Ruby variables: https://www.javatpoint.com/ruby-variables, accessed on August 24, 2022.
9. Global variable in Ruby: https://www.geeksforgeeks.org/global-variable-in-ruby/, accessed on August 24, 2022.
10. Ruby – comments: https://www.tutorialspoint.com/ruby/ruby_comments.htm, accessed on August 24, 2022.
11. Comments in Ruby: https://www.geeksforgeeks.org/comments-in-ruby/, accessed on August 24, 2022.
12. Ruby | Ranges: https://www.geeksforgeeks.org/ruby-ranges/, accessed on August 24, 2022.
13. Ruby – ranges: https://www.tutorialspoint.com/ruby/ruby_ranges.htm, accessed on August 24, 2022.
14. Ruby literals: https://www.geeksforgeeks.org/ruby-literals/, accessed on August 24, 2022.
15. Ruby literals: https://www.w3resource.com/ruby/ruby-literals.php, accessed on August 24, 2022.
16. Ruby directories: https://www.geeksforgeeks.org/ruby-directories/, accessed on August 25, 2022.

17. Ruby directories: https://www.javatpoint.com/ruby-directories, accessed on August 25, 2022.
18. Ruby | operators: https://www.geeksforgeeks.org/ruby-operators/, accessed on August 25, 2022.
19. Ruby – operators: https://www.tutorialspoint.com/ruby/ruby_operators.htm, accessed on August 25, 2022.
20. Operator precedence in Ruby: https://www.geeksforgeeks.org/operator-precedence-in-ruby/, accessed on August 25, 2022.
21. Operator overloading in Ruby: https://www.geeksforgeeks.org/operator-overloading-in-ruby/, accessed on August 25, 2022.
22. Ruby operator overloading: https://www.cosmiclearn.com/ruby/operatoro-verloading.php, accessed on August 25, 2022.
23. Ruby | Predefine variables and constants: https://www.geeksforgeeks.org/ruby-pre-define-variables-constants/, accessed on August 26, 2022.
24. Ruby | Unless statement and unless modifier: https://www.geeksforgeeks.org/ruby-unless-statement-and-unless-modifier/, accessed on August 26, 2022.
25. Unless statement and unless modifier in Ruby: https://www.tutorialspoint.com/unless-statement-and-unless-modifier-in-ruby#:~:text=We%20know%20that%20we%20can,condition%20that%20evaluates%20to%20False, accessed on August 26, 2022.

## CHAPTER 4

Control Statements in Ruby

IN THIS CHAPTER

- ➤ Decision-Making
- ➤ Loops
- ➤ Case Statement in Ruby
- ➤ Control Flow Alteration
- ➤ Break and Next Statement
- ➤ Redo and Retry Statement
- ➤ File Handling in Ruby

The last chapter discussed the fundamentals of Ruby, and this chapter will go through control statements in Ruby.

DECISION-MAKING (IF, IF-ELSE, IF-ELSE-IF, TERNARY) IN RUBY

Making decisions in programming is identical to making decisions in real life. A specific code section must perform when a given condition is met in programming. Control statements are used in computer languages to control the flow of execution of a program based on particular criteria.[1] These are used to trigger the execution flow to progress and branch according

DOI: 10.1201/9781003358510-4

to changes in a program's state. Likewise, the if-else expression in Ruby is used to test the given condition.

Ruby Decision-Making Statements

- if statement

- if-else statement

- if-else-if ladder

- ternary statement

If Statement
In Ruby, the if statement is used to determine if a specific statement or set of statements will perform or not, that is, if a given condition is true, then a block of statements is run; otherwise, not.[2]

Syntax:

```
if (condition)

    # statements to execute

end
```

Flowchart:

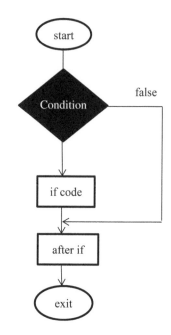

Statement of if.

Example:

```ruby
# program to illustrate the if statement

a = 30

# if condition to check whether
# our age is enough for the voting
if a >= 19
puts "We are eligible to vote."
end
```

If-Else Statement

When the condition is true, the "if" statement is used to run a block of code, and when the condition is not true, the "else" statement is used to perform a piece of code.[3]

Syntax:

```
if(condition)

    # code if condition is true

else

    # code if condition is false
end
```

Flowchart:

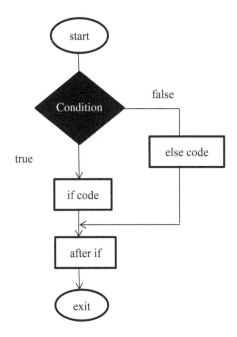

Statement of if-else.

Example:

```
# program to illustrate
# if - else statement

a = 22
```

```
# if condition to check
# whether age is enough for the voting
if a >= 19
puts "We are eligible to vote."
else
puts "We are not eligible to vote."
```

If-Else-If-Else Ladder Statement

A user can choose from several alternatives here, if statements are performed from the top down. When one of the criteria controlling the "if" is true, the statement associated with that "if" is performed, and the rest of the ladder is skipped. If none of the requirements are met, the last else statement is performed.

Syntax:

```
if(condition1)

# code to execute if the condition1 is true

elsif(condition2)

# code to execute if the condition2 is true

else(condition3)

# code to execute if the condition3 is true
end
```

Flowchart:

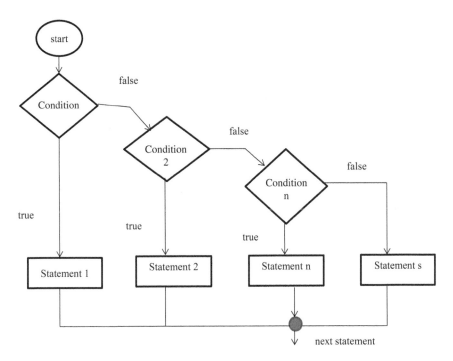

Statement of if-else-if.

Example:

```
# program to illustrate
# the if - else - if statement

m = 83
if m < 55
puts "Student is failed"

elsif m >= 55 && m <= 65
puts "The Student gets D grade"

elsif m >= 75 && m <= 88
puts "The Student gets B grade"

elsif m >= 85 && m <= 95
puts "The Student gets A grade"
```

```
elsif m >= 95 && m <= 100
puts "The Student gets A+ grade"
end
```

Ternary Statement

The ternary statement is also known as the shorter if statement in Ruby. It will first assess the expression to see if it is true or false and then run one of the statements. If the expression is true, the true statement is performed; else, the false statement is executed.

Syntax:

```
Test_expression?  if-true-expression :
if-false-expression
```

Example:

```
# program to illustrate
# the Ternary statement

# variable
var = 8;

# ternary statement
m = (var > 2)?  true : false ;
puts m
```

LOOPS (FOR, WHILE, DO..WHILE, UNTIL) IN RUBY

In computer languages, looping is a feature that allows the execution of a series of instructions or functions continuously when some of the conditions evaluate to true or false.[4] Ruby includes many forms of loops to handle conditional situations in programs, making the programmers' job easier. Ruby's loops are as follows:

- while loop

- for loop

- do..while loop

- until loop

While Loop

The condition to be tested is specified at the start of the loop, and all statements are run until the specified Boolean condition is satisfied. When the condition is met, the control will exit the while loop. Because the condition to be evaluated is present at the beginning of the loop body, it is also called an Entry Controlled Loop. So, in general, a while loop is used when the number of repetitions in a code is not fixed.

Syntax:

```
while conditional [do]

  # code to execute

end
```

The conditional in a while loop is separated from the code by the reserved word do, a newline, backslash (\), or a semicolon (;).

Flowchart:

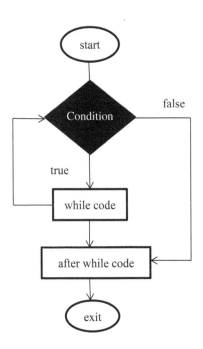

While loop.

Example:

```
# program to illustrate the 'while' loop

# variable m
m = 5

# using while loop
# here conditional is m i.e. 5
while m >= 1

# statements to be executed
puts "PeeksforPeeks"
m = m - 1

# while loop ends here
end
```

For Loop

The "for" loop performs similar functions to the while loop but has a distinct syntax. When the number of times loop statements are to be run is known ahead of time, a for loop is preferable. It iterates through a set of integers.[5] Because the condition to be evaluated is present at the beginning of the loop body, it is also called as an Entry Controlled Loop.

Syntax:

```
for variable-name [, variable...] in expression
[do]

    # code to execute

end
```

- for: A Ruby keyword that denotes the start of the loop.
- variable-name: This is a variable name that acts as a reference to the loop's current iteration.
- in: This is a Ruby keyword that is mostly used in for loops.
- expression: It runs code only once for each element in the expression. Expression can be a range or an array variable here.

- do: This denotes the start of the code block that will be performed repeatedly. It is optional to do.

- end: This keyword represents the end of the "for" loop block that began with the "do" keyword.

Example 1:

```
# program to illustrate 'for'
# loop using the range as expression

x = "Sudo Placements"

# using for loop with range
for a in 1..6 do

puts x

end
```

Explanation: We have specified the range 1..6 here. Range operators generate a sequence of values that includes a start, end, and a range of values in between. The (..) constructs a range that includes the final word. The expression for an in 1..6 allows a to take values ranging from 1 to 6 (including 6).

Example 2:

```
# program to illustrate 'for'
# loop using the array as expression

# array
arr = ["PFP", "P4P", "Peeks", "Sudo"]

# using for loop
for x in arr do

puts x

end
```

Do..While Loop

The do..while loop is identical to the while loop with the exception that it verifies the condition after running the statements, that is, it will only perform the loop body once. It is classified as an exit-controlled loop since it checks the condition that appears at the conclusion of the loop body.

Syntax:

```
loop do

  # code to execute

break if Boolean-Expression

end
```

Boolean expression will produce either a true or false output based on the comparing operators (>, =, <=, !=, ==). We can also use several Boolean expressions (Boolean expressions) within parentheses, which logical operators will join (&&, ||, !).

Example:

```
# program to illustrate the 'do..while' loop

# starting of the do..while loop
loop do

puts "PeeksforPeeks"

val = '7'

# using the Boolean expressions
if val == '7'
break
end

# ending of the ruby do..while loop
end
```

Until Loop

The until loop in Ruby executes statements or code till the specified condition is true. Essentially, it is the inverse of the while loop, which executes until the provided condition evaluates to false. The conditional in an until statement is divided from the program by the reserved word do, a newline, or a semicolon.

Syntax:

```
until conditional [do]

  # code to execute

end
```

Example:

```
# program to illustrate the 'until' loop

var = 7

# using the until loop
# here do is optional
until var == 12 do

# code to execute
puts var * 10
var = var + 2

# here loop ends
end
```

CASE STATEMENT IN RUBY

Like the switch statement in other languages, the case statement is a multiway branch statement. It allows us to easily route execution to various areas of code depending on the value of the expression.[6]

In the case statement, three critical keywords are used:

- case: It is identical to the switch keyword in other computer languages. It accepts the variables that the when keyword will utilize.

- when: In other computer languages, it is equivalent to the case key-word. It is only used to match one condition. A single case statement might include several when statements.

- else: It is analogous to the default keyword in other computer lan-guages. It is optional and will be executed if no matches are found.

Syntax:

```
case expression

when expression-1
  # our code

when expression-2
  # our code
  .

  .

  .
else
  # our code
end
```

First example:

```
# program to illustrate
# concept of the case statement

#!/usr/bin/ruby

print "Input from the one, two, three, four: "

# taking input from the user
# str = gets.chomp

# hardcoded input
str = "two"

# using the case statement
case str

# using when
```

```
when "one"
puts 'The Input is 1'

when "two"
puts 'The Input is 2'

when "three"
puts 'The Input is 3'

when "four"
puts 'The Input is 4'

else
puts "Default!"

end
```

Second example:

```
# program to illustrate
# the case statement

#!/usr/bin/ruby

marks = 80

# marks is the input
# for the case statement
case marks

# using the range operators..
when 0..34
puts "We fail!"

when 36..43
puts "We got C grade!"

when 44..69
puts "We got B grade!"

else
puts "We got A grade!"

end
```

Important Notes

- The when statement, like the case statement, can have different values and ranges (see the above example).

Example:

```
# program to illustrate
# how to use the multiple values
# in when statement

choice = "5"

# using 'case' statement
case choice

    # here 'when' statement contains the
    # two values
    when "1","2"
        puts "We order Espresso!"

    when "3","4"
        puts "We order Short Macchiato!"

    when "5","6"
        puts "We order Ristretto!"

    when "7","8"
        puts "We order Cappuccino!"

else
    "No Order!"
end
```

- We may also use a case statement that has no value.

Example:

```
# program to illustrate no
# value in the case statement

str = "PeeksforPeeks"

# here case statement
```

```
# has no value
case

    # using the match keyword to check
    when str.match(/\d/)
        puts 'The String contains numbers'

    when str.match(/[a-zA-Z]/)
        puts 'The String contains letters'
else
    puts 'String does not contain the numbers &
letters'
end
```

In a method call, we can utilize a case statement. A case statement, like a method call, will always return a single object.

Example:

```
# program to illustrate case
# statement in the method call

str = "1234"

# case statement here
# has no value & used as
# in puts method call
puts case

    # using the match keyword to check
    when str.match(/\d/)

        'The String contains numbers'

    when str.match(/[a-zA-Z]/)

        'The String contains letters'
else

    'The String does not contain numbers &
letters'
end
```

CONTROL FLOW ALTERATION IN RUBY

In contrast to loops, conditionals, and iterators, the Ruby computer program has several statements for modifying the control process of a code.

In other words, these statements are codes that are executed one after the other until the condition is met, at which point the code exits. The following statements can change the control flow in a Ruby program:

- break statement

- next statement

- redo statement

- retry statement

- return statement

- throw/catch statement

Break Statement

When the condition is true, the Break statement in Ruby is used to end the loop. Break statements are commonly used in while loops because the output is displayed until the condition is true and the loop exits when the condition is false. Within the loop, the break statement is utilized. The break keyword is used to execute the break statement. For, while, and case-control statements can all employ the break statement.

Syntax:

```
break
```

Example:

```
# program to illustrate the break statement

#!/usr/bin/ruby

m = 1

# using the while loop
while true
```

```
if m * 7 >= 35

    # using the break statement
    break

  # ending of the if statement
  end

  puts m * 7
  m += 1

# ending of the while loop
end
```

Next Statement

The next statement in Ruby is used to access the next iterator in a specified loop. In C and Java, the next statement is the same as the continue statement. When the following sentence is used, no more iterations are done. The next statement is commonly used in for and while loops.

Syntax:

```
next
```

Example:

```
# program to illustrate the next statement

#!/usr/bin/ruby

# using the for loop
for t in 0...11

# using the if statement
if t == 6 then

    # using the next statement
    next

# ending of if
end
```

```
# display values
puts t

# end of the for loop
end
```

Redo Statement

The redo command is used to resume the current loop or iterator iteration. There is a distinction between the redo and the following sentence. The next statement always sends control to the conclusion of the loop, where the statement following the loop may begin to run, whereas the redo statement returns control to the top of the block or loop, where iteration can begin again.

Syntax:

```
redo
```

Example:

```
# program to demonstrate redo statement

# define a variable
val = 0

# using the while loop which should
give output
# as 0,1,2,3 but here
# it will output as 0,1,2,3,4
while(val < 4)

# here Control returns when
# redo will execute
puts val
val += 1

# using the redo statement
redo if val == 4

# ending of the while loop
end
```

Explanation: In the above code, the redo command transfers control to puts val, which is the first expression in the while loop. It will not recheck the loop condition or get the next component from the iterator. As a result, the while loop here will display 0, 1, 2, 3, 4 instead of 0, 1, 2, 3.

Retry Statement (Deprecated in Recent Versions)

The retry statement is utilized to restart an iterator depending on a condition or any method call from the beginning. Simply put, the retry statement returns control to the beginning. A retry statement is rarely used in practice.[7] It will only work till Ruby 1.8.

The retry statement has been removed from Ruby versions 1.9 and beyond since it is a deprecated language feature.[8] As a result, it will almost never run on online IDEs because most of them utilize versions higher than 1.8.

Syntax:

```
retry
```

Example:

```
# program to demonstrate retry statement

# variable
var = 7

# Iterate 7 times from the 0 to 7-1
var.times do |val|

# display the iteration number
puts val

# If we have reached 6
if val == 6

# Decrement the val and user
# won't reach 6 next time
var = var - 1

# Restart iteration
# using the retry statement
```

```
retry

# end of if
end

# end of do..end
end
```

Explanation: In the preceding code, when the control is transferred to the retry statement, it is transferred to var.times do |val|. The value of the var variable is now updated, that is, 5. As a result, the user will not reach 6 the following time, and the retry statement will not execute again.

Return Statement

This method is used to quit a method with or without a value. It always gives its caller a value. The return statement has several alternatives. The method's value is always returned as nil if no expression is provided with the return statement. Following the return statement, a list of expressions is always divided by a comma (,). The method's value in this scenario will be an array containing the values of the provided expressions.

Example:

```
# program to demonstrate return statement

#!/usr/bin/ruby

# defining a method 'peeks'
def peeks

# variables of the method
val1 = 72
val2 = 44

# returning multiple values
return val1, val2

# this statement will not execute
puts "Hello Peeks"

# end of method
end
```

```
# variable outside method to
# store return value of the method
value = peeks

# display the returned values
puts value
```

Explanation: In the preceding example, method peeks include a return statement that returns two values to its caller, val1 and val2. The variable value is used to hold the returned values. The essential aspect is that the line after the return statement that says "Hello Peeks" does not execute because statements after the return statement do not execute within a method.

Throw/Catch Statement

Throw and catch are used to characterize a control structure that may be considered a multilevel break. The throw keyword is used to break the current loop and move control outside of the catch block. The nicest part about toss is that it can exit the current loop or procedures or span any number of levels. In this case, catch specifies a "labeled block" of code that triggers the throw block to exit.

Example:

```
# program to illustrate throw/catch statement
# for altering control flow

# define a method
def lessNumber(num)

    # using the throw statement
    # here 'numberError' is its label
    throw :numberError if num < 12

    # display result
    puts "Number is Greater than 12!"
end

# catch block
catch :numberError do

    # calling method
    lessNumber(13)
    lessNumber(75)
```

```
    # exits catch block here
    lessNumber(6)
    lessNumber(3)
end

puts "Outside Catch Block"
```

Explanation: In the above program, 13 is supplied to method lessNumber to determine whether it is bigger than 12. Because 13 is more than 12, the statement will be printed on the screen and the following statement in the catch block will execute. Now, 75 is supplied to the method call, which is examined, and if it is more than 12, the statement is printed on the screen. However, if 6 is provided, which is less than 12, throw: numberError, causing the catch block to leave and all lines to skip out, with the last statement printing "Outside Catch Block." As a result, as soon as the condition turns false, throw triggers the catch block to terminate execution.

BREAK AND NEXT STATEMENT IN RUBY

To break the processing of the loop in the program, we utilize a break statement in Ruby.[9] It is typically used in while loops, where the value is presented until the condition is fulfilled, at which time the loop is terminated by the break statement.

Syntax:

```
Break
```

Example:

```
# program to use break statement
#!/usr/bin/ruby -w

x = 1

# Using the While Loop
while true

    # Print Values
    puts x * 3
```

```
x += 1
if x * 3 >= 21

    # Using the Break Statement
    break
end
end
```

In the instances, the break statement is used with an if statement. The execution will be halted by utilizing the break statement. In the preceding example, if x * 3 is more than 21, execution will be terminated.

Example:

```
# Ruby program to use break statement

#!/usr/bin/ruby -w

m = 0

    # Using while
    while true do

        # Print Value
        puts m
        m += 1

    # Using the Break Statement
    break if m > 3
end
```

The above program limits the number of loop iterations to three.

Next Statement

We utilize the next statement to skip the rest of the current iteration. When the following statement is executed, no more iteration is done.[10] In every other language, the next statement is equivalent to the continue statement.

Syntax:

```
next
```

Example:

```
# program of using next statement
#!/usr/bin/ruby -w

for m in 0..6

        # Used condition
        if m+1 < 4 then

            # Using next statement
            next
        end

        # Print values
        puts "The Value of m is : #{m}"
    end
```

In the above instance, the value is not printed until the condition is met, at which point the iteration proceeds to the next. When the condition is false, the value of *m* is displayed.

THE REDO AND RETRY STATEMENT IN RUBY

Let's discuss redo and retry statement in brief.

Redo Statement

The redo command in Ruby is used to repeat the current iteration of the loop. Inside the loop, redo is always utilized.[11] The redo statement repeats the loop but does not reevaluate the condition.

```
# program of using the redo statement

#!/usr/bin/ruby
restart = false

# Using the for loop
for m in 2..22
    if m == 17
        if restart == false

            # Print values
            puts "Re-doing when m = " + m.to_s
            restart = true
```

```
            # Using the Redo Statement
            redo
        end
    end
    puts m
end
```

Retry Statement

The retry statement is used to restart the loop iteration from the beginning.[12] Retry is always utilized within the loop.

First example:

```
# program of retry statement

# Using the do loop
10.times do |x|
begin
    puts "Iteration #{x}"
    raise if x > 2
rescue

    # Using the retry
    retry
end
end
```

Second example:

```
# program of retry statement
def peeks
attempt_again = true
p 'checking'
begin

    # This is point where control flow jumps
    p 'crash'
    raise 'foo'
    rescue Exception => e
        if attempt_again
        attempt_again = false
```

```
      # Using the retry
      retry
      end
  end
  end
```

BEGIN AND END BLOCKS IN RUBY

Every Ruby source code can execute the BEGIN blocks when the file is loaded and the END blocks when the code is done. The BEGIN and END statements are distinct from one another. BEGIN and END blocks might appear many times in a code.[13] If a program has more than one BEGIN statement, they are run in the order listed. If there are several END statements, they are performed in reverse order. The first END is carried out last. An open curly brace is usually placed between the BEGIN and END keywords.[14]

Syntax:

```
BEGIN{
    Code
    . . .
    .}
    END{
    . . .
    .}
```

Example:

```
# Program of the BEGIN and END Block

BEGIN {
# BEGIN block code
puts "the BEGIN code block"
}

END {
# END block code
puts "The END code block"
}
# MAIN block code
puts "PeeksForPeeks"
```

As seen in the above case, the BEGIN block code is run first, followed by the Main block code, and finally by the END block code.

Example:

```
# Program of the BEGIN and END Block

# BEGIN block
BEGIN {

d = 4
e = 3
f = d + e

# BEGIN block code
puts "This is the BEGIN block code"
puts f

}

# END block
END {

d = 4
e = 3
f = d * e

# END block code
puts "This is the END block code"
puts f
}

# the Code will execute before END block
puts "Main Block"
```

FILE HANDLING IN RUBY

It is a method of processing a file that includes the following operations: generating a new file, reading content from a file, writing content to a file, appending content to a file, renaming the file, and removing the file.[15]

Common file handling modes

- "r": indicates that a file is in read-only mode.

- "r+:" indicates that a file is in read-write mode.

- "w": a file's write-only mode.

- "w+" indicates that a file is in read-write mode.

- "a": write-only mode; if the file already exists, the data will append; otherwise, a new file will create.

- "a+": read and write mode; if the file already exists, the data will append; otherwise, a new file is created.

  ```
  Making a new file
  Depending on the mode string, we may build a new
  File using the File.new() method for reading,
  writing, or both. To close that file, we may
  utilize the fileobject.close() function.

  Making changes to the file
  We can write data to a file using the syswrite
  technique. This method requires that the file be
  opened in write mode. The new content will
  overwrite the current content in an existing file.
  ```

Syntax:

```
fileobject = File.new("file_name.txt", "mode")
fileobject.syswrite("Text to write into file")
fileobject.close()
```

Example:

```
# Program of File Handling

# Create a file
fileobject = File.new("sample1.txt", "w+");

# Write to the file
fileobject.syswrite("File Handling");

# Close a file
fileobject.close();
```

A text file called sample.txt is created with read and write permissions. Using the syswrite method, the content "File Handling" is written to the file. Lastly, save the file. When we open the sample.txt file, the string "File Handling" will appear.[16]

Syntax:

```
fileobject = File.new("filename1.txt", "r")
fileobject.sysread(22)
fileobject.close()
```

Example:

```
# Program of File Handling

# Opene a file
fileobject = File.open("sample1.txt", "r");

# Read first n characters from a file
puts(fileobject.sysread(22));

# Close a file
fileobject.close();

# Open a file
fileobject = File.open("sample1.txt", "r");

# Read values as an array of lines
print(fileobject.readlines);
puts

# Close a file
fileobject.close();

# Open a file
fileobject = File.open("sample1.txt", "r");

# Read entire content from a file
print(fileobject.read());

# Close a file
fileobject.close();
```

The string "File handling in Ruby language" appears in the example text file. The file has been opened with read-only permissions. The result shown above demonstrates several methods for reading and printing files. The sysread function reads just 22 characters and prints the first 22. The values were read as an array of lines via the read-lines method. The read method reads the whole contents of the file as a string.

```
# Rename file name
puts File.rename("sample1.txt", "newSample.txt")

# Delete existing file
puts File.delete("sample2.txt")

# Check the old filename is existing or not
puts File.file?("sample1.txt")

# Check the renamed file is exiting or not
puts File.file?("newSample1.txt")

# Check the file have read permission
puts File.readable?("newSample1.txt")

# Check the file have write permission
puts File.writable?("newSample1.txt")
```

The rename method is used to replace the old name in the file with the new name, and the rename method prints "0" if the file is successfully renamed, else it prints "1." The delete method is used to destroy the current file, and it will display "1" if the file is successfully destroyed, else it will print "0." The file? method is used to determine whether or not a file exists. If the file does not exist, it will return false; otherwise, it will return true. Because we renamed the sample.txt text file to newSample1. txt, it does not exist in our situation; hence, it returns false. Because the newSample1 file exists, it will return true. Because the newSample1 file has both read and write permissions, it will return true for the final two statements.

This chapter will explore decision-making statements, loops, case statements, and control flow alteration. In addition, we will go over the break and next statements, the redo and retry statements, and file handling in Ruby.

NOTES

1. Ruby | Decision-making (if, if-else, if-else-if, ternary) | Set 1: https://www.geeksforgeeks.org/ruby-decision-making-if-if-else-if-else-if-ternary-set-1/, accessed on August 26, 2022.
2. Ruby – if…else, case, unless: https://www.tutorialspoint.com/ruby/ruby_if_else.htm, accessed on August 26, 2022.
3. Ruby if-else statement: https://www.javatpoint.com/ruby-if-else, accessed on August 26, 2022.
4. Ruby | Loops (for, while, do…while, until): https://www.geeksforgeeks.org/ruby-loops-for-while-do-while-until/, accessed on August 26, 2022.
5. Loops and iterators: https://launchschool.com/books/ruby/read/loops_iterators, accessed on August 26, 2022.
6. Ruby | Case statement: https://www.geeksforgeeks.org/ruby-case-statement/, accessed on August 26, 2022.
7. Ruby | Control flow alteration: https://www.geeksforgeeks.org/ruby-control-flow-alteration/, accessed on August 26, 2022.
8. Control flow alterations in Ruby: https://www.tutorialspoint.com/control-flow-alterations-in-ruby, accessed on August 26, 2022.
9. Ruby break and next statement: https://www.geeksforgeeks.org/ruby-break-and-next-statement/, accessed on August 27, 2022.
10. Ruby break statement: https://www.javatpoint.com/ruby-break-and-next-statement, accessed on August 27, 2022.
11. Ruby redo and retry statement: https://www.geeksforgeeks.org/ruby-redo-and-retry-statement/, accessed on August 27, 2022.
12. Redo and retry statements in Ruby: https://www.includehelp.com/ruby/redo-and-retry-statements.aspx, accessed on August 27, 2022.
13. BEGIN and END blocks in Ruby: https://www.geeksforgeeks.org/begin-and-end-blocks-in-ruby/, accessed on August 27, 2022.
14. How to use Ruby BEGIN and END blocks: https://scoutapm.com/blog/ruby-begin-end#:~:text=Conclusion-,What%20are%20Ruby%20BEGIN%20and%20END%20Blocks%3F,position%20in%20the%20source%20file, accessed on August 27, 2022.
15. File handling in Ruby: https://www.geeksforgeeks.org/file-handling-in-ruby/, accessed on August 27, 2022.
16. Ruby file handling: https://www.studytonight.com/ruby/file-handling-in-ruby, accessed on August 27, 2022.

## CHAPTER 5

Methods in Ruby

IN THIS CHAPTER

- ➢ Methods
- ➢ Recursion in Ruby
- ➢ Hook Methods in Ruby
- ➢ Range Class Methods
- ➢ Initialize Method
- ➢ Method Overriding
- ➢ Date and Time

In the previous chapter, we covered control statements in Ruby, and in this chapter, we will discuss methods in Ruby.

METHODS IN RUBY

A method is a set of statements that complete a certain task and give the result. Methods save time by allowing the user to reuse code without having to retype it. Define and call the method: In Ruby, the method is defined with the def keyword, followed by the method_name, and finally with the end keyword.[1] A method must declare before it may be called, and its name must be in lowercase. Methods are simply referred to by their names. When calling a method, just write the name of the method.

DOI: 10.1201/9781003358510-5

Syntax:

```
def method-name
# Statement-1
# Statement-2
.
.
end
```

Example:

```
# program to illustrate defining
# and calling of the method

#!/usr/bin/ruby

# Here peeks is the method name
def peeks

# statements to display
puts "Welcome to PFP portal"

# keyword to end method
end

# calling of method
peeks
```

Passing Parameters to Methods

Parameter passing in Ruby is identical to parameter passing in other computer languages because the arguments are simply written in brackets ( ).

Syntax:

```
def method-name(var1, var2, var3)
# Statement-1
# Statement-2
.
.
end
```

Example:

```
# program to illustrate the
# parameter passing to methods

#!/usr/bin/ruby

# peeks is the method name
# var1 and var2 are parameters
def geeks (var1 = "PFP", var2 = "P4P")

    # statements to execute
    puts "The First parameter is #{var1}"
    puts "The First parameter is #{var2}"
end

# calling method with the parameters
peeks "PeeksforPeeks", "Sudo"

puts ""

puts "Without Parameters"
puts ""

# calling method without passing the parameters
peeks
```

Variable Number of Parameters

Ruby allows programmers to design methods that accept a variable number of parameters. It is useful when the user does not know how many arguments should be provided while defining the method.[2]

Syntax:

```
def method-name (*variable-name)
# Statement-1
# Statement-2
 .
 .
 .
end
```

Example:

```
# program to illustrate method that
# takes variables number of arguments
```

```
#!/usr/bin/ruby

# define method peeks that can
# take any number of the arguments
def peeks (*var)

# to display total number of the parameters
puts "The Number of parameters is: #{var.length}"

# using the for loop
for x in 0...var.length
    puts "Parameters are: #{var[x]}"
end
end

# call method by passing
# variable number of the arguments
peeks "PFP", "P4P"
peeks "PeeksforPeeks"
```

Return Statement in Methods

The return statement returns one or more values. By default, a method usually returns the last statement evaluated in the method's body. To return the statements, utilize the "return" keyword.

Example:

```
# program to illustrate the method return
statement

#!/usr/bin/ruby

# peeks is method name
def num

# variables of the method
m = 20
n = 44

sum = m + n

# return value of the sum
return sum
```

```
end

# calling of the num method
puts "Result is: #{num}"
```

METHOD VISIBILITY IN RUBY

In Ruby, method visibility relates to whether instance methods are public, private, or protected. Unless expressly defined private or protected, methods are by default public.[3] In Ruby, method visibility is used to accomplish Data Abstraction, or to reveal just necessary information while hiding background data.

In Ruby, method visibility is determined by one of three types of access modifiers:

- Public access modifier

- Protected access modifier

- Private access modifier

Public Access Modifier

The public methods of a class can invoke from anywhere in the code.

Example:

```
# program to illustrate the public access modifier

# define class
class Peeks

    # methods are public by default
    def publicMethod_1
        puts "publicMethod1 called!"
    end

    # using the public keyword
    public

    def publicMethod_2
        puts "publicMethod2 called!"
    end

end
```

```
# create the object
objt = Peeks.new()

# call methods
objt.publicMethod_1()
objt.publicMethod_2()
```

The given code calls two public methods of the class Peeks, public-Method_1() and publicMethod_2().

Protected Access Modifier

Methods defined protected in a class can only be invoked from the class in which they are defined and classes derived from it.[4]

Example:

```
# program to illustrate the protected access
modifier

# the super class
class Parent

    # the protected keyword
    protected
# The protected method
# cannot call directly
def protected_Method
        puts "protected_Method called!"
    end

end

# sub class
class Peeks < Parent

def public_Method
    # protected method called in the public method
    self.protected_Method
end

end
```

```
# create object
obj = Peeks.new

# call method
obj.public_Method
```

Because the protected_Method() of the Parent class is not directly available in the above code, it is called from the public_Method() of the derived class Peeks.

Private Access Modifier

The methods of a class that are designated private are only invoked within the class; the private access modifier is the most safe.

Example:

```
# program to illustrate the private access
modifier

# defining class
class Peeks

    # the private keyword
    private
# private method
# cannot call directly
def private_Method
        puts "private_Method called!"
end
# the public keyword
public
# public method
def public_Method
    # private method called in public method
    private_Method
end

end

# create object
obj = peeks.new
```

```
# call method
obj.public_Method
```

The private_Method() method of the Peeks class is not invoked directly in the preceding code. So, it is invoked from the public_Method() of the class Peeks.

Let's have a look at another program that illustrates Method Visibility.

```
# program to illustrate the Method Visibility

# super class
class Parent

private
# private method
def private_Method
    puts "private_Method called!"
end

protected
# protected method
def protected_Method
        puts "protected_Method called!"
    end

public

# public methods
def public_Method1
    puts "public_Method1 called!"
end
def public_Method2
    # protected method called in public method
    protected_Method
    # private method called in public method
    private_Method
end

end

# sub class
class Child < Parent
```

```
# public method
def public_Method3
    # protected method called in public method
    protected-Method
end

end

# create object
obj1 = Parent.new
obj2 = Child.new

# call method
puts "\nParent methods: \n"
obj1.public_Method1
obj1.public_Method2
puts "\nChild methods: \n"
obj2.public_Method1
obj2.public_Method3
```

RECURSION IN RUBY

Recursion is the procedure through which a function directly or indirectly calls itself, and the accompanying function is referred to as a recursive function. Recursion simplifies the procedure and significantly saves compilation time. In Ruby, we have the option of looping all of the activities so that they may be performed an infinite number of times. So, why is Recursion required?

Recursion is crucial in solving large real-life problems in Ruby since we introduce real-life variables.[5]

Simple code: We may comprehend the steps by examining a very simple problem of array adding. Iterative code would include looping through the array, adding each piece to a variable, and then returning the variable.

Example:

```
# Iterative program to execute summing of given
array of the numbers.
def iterativeSum(arrayofNumbers)
sum = 0
arrayofNumbers.each do |number|
    sum += number
```

```
end
    sum
end

iterativeSum([11, 7, 2, 8, 4, 5, 6, 9, 3, 10])
```

Writing Recursive Code

The procedure calls itself in this code. The solution to the base case is supplied in the recursive algorithm, and the answer to the larger problem is represented in terms of small issues.

Example:

```
# Recursive method to calculate sum of all numbers
in given array.
def RecursiveSum(arrayofNumbers)
# Base Case: If array is empty, return 0.
return 0 if arrayofNumbers.empty?

# Recursive code: Adding each element to variable
by calling method.
sum = arrayofNumbers.pop
return sum + RecursiveSum(arrayofNumbers)
end

RecursiveSum([11, 22, 31, 43, 15, 68, 72, 87, 91, 10])
```

Another example may use to see how the Recursive steps are successfully carried out. In the instance below, we would run a simple code to discover the Factorial of a given integer.

The following is the code for the previously described program:

```
# Ruby program, for calculating factorial of number
recursively.

def RecursiveFactorial(number)

# Base Case:

if (0..1).include?(number)
    return 1
end
```

```
#Recursive call:

    number * RecursiveFactorial(number - 1)
end
# Call the method:

RecursiveFactorial(7)
```

A program for computing the Nth Fibonacci number is another example. In this example, the base case occurs when N is smaller than 2 because the Fibonacci number is itself. The recursive call would be calling the procedure for computing the $(n - 1)$th and $(n - 2)$nd Fibonacci numbers and adding them to get the answer for the Nth number.

Example:

```
# program for calculating Nth Fibonacci number.
def Fibonacci(number)

# Base case : when N is less than 3.
if number < 3
    number
else

    # Recursive call : sum of the last two
Fibonacci's.
    Fibonacci(number - 1) + Fibonacci(number - 2)
end
end

Fibonacci(4)
```

When calculating through the Iterative process, the notion of Recursion addresses numerous difficulties and simplifies the process. Thus, if one understands the notion of recursion, one may solve numerous issues in less time and with less lines of code. When a huge integer is used as an input, Recursion in Ruby occasionally returns "SystemStackError: stack level too deep" (this number varies with the system). This indicates that we'd have to take an iterative approach to an issue with many inputs.

HOOK METHODS IN RUBY

Ruby hook methods are invoked as a result of something you do. They are typically used to enhance the functionality of methods during run time. These methods are not specified by default, but a coder may declare them to imply them on any object, class, or module, and they will be called when specific events occur.[6]

When methods are invoked, subclasses of a class are established, or modules are added, these methods serve to expand the behavior of basics. The Ruby language's meta-programming capability enables users to construct dynamic code at run time with ease.

Once a specific action has been performed, the hook methods can execute a particular function.

There are various Ruby hook methods; however, the following serve important roles:

- Included

- Prepended

- Extended

- Inherited

- method_missing

Modules in Ruby

Before proceeding with the methods, it is necessary to grasp the idea of modules in Ruby. Modules are just groups of code that may be created once and used several times. Hook methods are often used to retrieve and modify them.

Included

This method adds a method, attribute, or module to another module. The method makes the underlined module accessible to the class's instances. The included function is demonstrated and explained in the following instance.

The program in the instance generates a remark when the module is invoked in the class where it is included.

```
# Declare a module to greet person
module Greetings
```

```
def self.included(person_to_be_greeted)

    puts "The #{person_to_be_greeted} is welcomed with
open heart !"
end
end

# Class where module is included
class Person

include Greetings # implementation of include
statement
end
```

Prepended

Ruby 2.0 introduced this method. This differs somewhat from what we saw earlier. The prepended technique adds another means to expand the functionality of modules at multiple locations. This makes use of the idea of overriding. Methods specified in the target class can use to override the modules.

The following self-explanatory instance can help us understand the Prepended method:

```
# Code as an example for the prepend method
module Ruby

def self.prepended(target) # Implementation of the
prepend method
    puts "#{self} has been prepended to #{target}"
end

def Type
    "Type belongs to Ruby"
end
end

class Coding

prepend Ruby # module Ruby is prepended
end

# Method call
puts Coding.new.Type
```

Extended

This approach is distinct from the include-and-prepend methods. While include applies methods from a certain module to a class instance, extend applies those methods to the same class.

The program as mentioned above may be executed using the extend method as follows:

```ruby
# Code as an example for the extend method
module Ruby

def self.extended(target)
    puts "#{self} was extended by the #{target}"
end

def Type
    "Type is Ruby"
end
end


class Coding

extend Ruby # Extending module Ruby
end

# the Method calling
puts Coding.Type
```

Inherited

Inheritance is a fundamental notion in object-oriented programming and is found in practically every computer language. Because we are dealing with things inspired by the real world in Ruby, oops methods are particularly crucial. When a subclass of a class is implemented, the inherited method is invoked. It's a method for making a child class from a parent class.

The following example demonstrates this:

```ruby
# Making parent Vehicles class
class Vehicles

def self.inherited(car_type)
    puts "#{car_type} is a kind of the Vehicles"
end

end
```

```
# the Target class
class Hyundai < Vehicles #Inhereting the Vehicles
class
end
```

method_missing

The method missing method is one of the most commonly used in Ruby. This occurs when attempting to invoke a method on an object that does not exist.

The following instance demonstrates how it works:

```
# main class
class Ruby

def method_missing(input, *args) # method_missing
function in the action
    "#{input} not defined on the #{self}"
end

def Type
    "Type is Ruby"
end
end

var = Ruby.new

# Call a method that exists
puts var.Type

# Call a method that does not exist
puts var.Name
```

The callback idea is sometimes confused with the hook methods. While callbacks are source code pieces like as methods, modules, and so on, a hook is just a location in the code where they are accessible. As a result, the idea of callback should not be confused with Ruby hooks.

As we all know, the Ruby computer language has a very explicit correlation with everyday objects and methods; thus, anybody working in the language must have a complete understanding of all the necessary oops notions, and hook methods are one of them.

RANGE CLASS METHODS IN RUBY

Ruby has a Range class. Ruby ranges represent a set of values with a start and an end point. A range's values can be integers, characters, strings, or objects. It is built with start_point...end_point, start_point...end_point literals, or with::new. It adds flexibility to the code while also reducing its size. Range.new can also use to build a range.[7] A range that contains (two dots) runs from the starting value to the end value inclusively, but a range that contains (three dots) excludes the final value.

Example:

```
(1..7).to_a     # Output= [1, 2, 3, 4, 5, 6, 7]
(1...7).to_a    # Output= [1, 2, 3, 4, 5, 6]
```

Ranges can be generated in Ruby using objects as long as the objects can be compared using their <=> operator. It supports the succ function in order to return the following item in succession.

Class Method

new: This method generates a range based on the start and finish values provided. The range comprises end-object if the third parameter is false or excluded in this method. Otherwise, it will leave out.

```
Range.new(start, end, exclusive=false)
```

Example:

```
# program to illustrate
# new Method

m = 12
n = 17

# Output will be 12..17
Range.new(m, n, false)
```

Instance Methods

==: This function returns true if obj has the same starting, ending, and third parameter value as rng. If not, it will return false. This method's return type is Boolean.

```
rng==obj-->true or false
```

Example:

```
# program to illustrate the
# use of == method

# Using the Range.new class method
m = Range.new(2, 6, false)
n = Range.new(2, 6, false)

# Using == instance method
m == n
```

===: If rng omits its end, this method returns rng.start <= value rng. end, and if rng is inclusive, it returns rng.start <= value <= rng.end. Usually, the comparison operator === is used in case statements.

```
rng===value --> true or false
```

Example:

```
# program to illustrate the use
# of === method by the case statement

# taking the case statement
case 25.67

when 1...56 then puts "Lower"
when 56...86 then puts "Medium"
when 86...100 then puts "Upper"
end
```

begin: This function returns the first rng object.

```
rng.begin --> obj
```

Example:

```
# program to illustrate the
# use of begin method

# Create range using new method
m = Range.new(4, 8, false)
```

```
# using the begin instance method
m.begin
```

each: This function is used to iterate through rng components by providing each one to the block in turn.

```
rng.each{|j| block} --> rng
```

Example:

```
# program to illustrate the
# use of each method

# using each method
(41..46).each do |x|
print x, '....'
end
```

end: This function returns the rng's end object.[8]

```
rng.end --> obj
```

Example:

```
# program to illustrate the
# use of end method

# using the end method
m = Range.new(2, 8, false)
m.end
```

eql?: This method determines if obj and rng are the same in regards of
start, finish, and exclusive flag. If obj has the same start, end, and exclusive
flag values as rng, it returns true; else, it returns false.

```
rng.eql?(obj) --> true or false
```

Example:

```
# program to illustrate the
# use of eql? method
```

```
# Constructing the ranges
m = Range.new(2, 6, false)
n = Range.new(2, 6, false)

# using eql? method
m.eql?(n)
```

exclude_end?: If the end of the rng is missing, this function returns true; otherwise, it returns false.

```
rng.exclude_end? --> true or false
```

Example:

```
# program to illustrate
# the use of exclude_end? method

# constructing the range
m = Range.new(3, 8, false)

# using the exclude_end? method
m.exclude_end?
```

first: This function returns the rng's beginning object.

```
rng.first --> obj
```

Example:

```
# program to illustrate the
# use of first method

# constructing the range
m = Range.new(3, 8, false)

# using first method
m.first
```

last: This function returns the last rng object.

```
rng.last --> obj
```

Example:

```
# program to illustrate the
# use of last method

# constructing the range
m = Range.new(3, 8, false)

# using the last method
m.last
```

member?: This method determines whether the provided value is a member of rng. If the provided value is a rng member, it returns true; else, it returns false.

```
rng.member?(value) --> true or false
```

Example:

```
# program to illustrate the
# use of member? method

# taking a range
m = 1..9

# using member? method
m.member?(4)
```

include?: If obj is an element of rng, this function returns true; else, it returns false.

```
rng.include?(value) --> true or false
```

Example:

```
# program to illustrate the
# use of include? method

# using the include? method
("A".."F").include?("Z")
```

step: This function iterates through rng, sending the *n*th item to the block. If the range comprises numbers, adding one to one results in a series of items. Instead, step invokes the succ function to iterate through the items in the range.

```
rng.step(n=1){|obj|block} --> rng
```

THE INITIALIZE METHOD IN RUBY

We may utilize the initialize method when we need to initialize certain class variables at the moment of object creation.[9] The initialize function in Ruby is part of the object-creation process and allows us to set an object's initial properties.

The following are some initialize-related points:

- We can provide the default argument.

- Because it always returns a new object, the return keyword is not utilized within the initialize method.

- If our class does not require any parameters, we do not need to use the initialize keyword.

- We will get an error if we try to send parameters into new and do not define initialize.

Syntax:

```
def initialize(argument-1, argument-2, .....)
```

Without the Variable Initialize

Example:

```
# program of Initialize method
class Peeks

# Method with the initialize keyword
def initialize(name)
end
end
```

In the above instance, we add a method named initialize to the class, with a single parameter name. The initialize method is used to create an object.

With the Initialize Variable

Example:

```
# program of Initialize method
class Rectangle

# Method with the initialize keyword
def initialize(m, n)

    # Initialize variable
    @m = m
    @n = n
end
end

# create new Rectangle instance by the calling
Rectangle.new(20, 10)
```

In the preceding instance, initialize variables are accessed within the class using the @ operator, but we will use public methods to access them outside of the class.

METHOD OVERRIDING IN RUBY

A method is a collection of statements that perform a certain task and return the result. Override refers to two methods with the same name but performing distinct duties. It signifies that one of the procedures takes precedence over another.[10] If there is a method in the superclass and a method with the same name in its subclass, then running these methods will perform the method of the appropriate class.

Example:

```
# program of method overriding

# define class
class X
def x
    puts 'Peeks'
end
end
```

```
# define subclass
class Y < X

# change existing method as follows
def x
    puts 'Welcome to PeeksForPeeks'
end
end

y = Y.new
y.x
```

In the above instance, a performance on the object of A printed Geeks from the x method is specified in the X class, but the execution of x on the object of Y printed Peeks from the x method is written in the Y class. Welcome to PeeksForPeeks from the Y class's method. It is quite beneficial since it keeps us from creating methods with various names and remembering them all.[11] The method in class B takes precedence over the method x in class X.

Example:

```
# program of method overriding

# define class
class Box
# the constructor method
def initialize(width, height)
    @wd, @ht = width, height
end
# instance method
def getArea
    @wd * @ht
end
end

# define subclass
class BigBox < Box

# change the existing getArea method as follows
def getArea
    @area = @wd * @ht
```

```
      puts "The Big box area is : #@area"
end
end

# create object
box = BigBox.new(26, 12)

# print area using the overridden method.
box.getArea()
```

The method getArea in class BigBox overrides the method getArea in class Box in the preceding instance.

DATE AND TIME IN RUBY

Ruby's Time and Date lesson deals with dates and times. It allows us to obtain the current time and date based on our system parameters. It also provides us with the components of a date and time, as well as the ability to format time and date.[12]

The date is a number that represents a day of the month or year. A date is made up of a month, a year, and a date. Date objects are generated using functions such as ::new, ::parse, ::today, ::jd, ::strptime, ::ordinal, ::commercial, and so on. All of the date objects are fixed.

Obtaining the Current Date and Time

Example:

```
time1 = Time.new
puts "The Current Time : " + time1.inspect
```

The above example uses the inspect method to obtain the current date and time.

Obtaining Date and Time Components

The time object may use to obtain various date and time elements.

Example:

```
# program to getting Date and Time
time = Time.new

# Components of Time
puts "Current Time :"+ time.inspect
```

```
puts time.year # => Year of date
puts time.month # => Month of date (1 to 12)
puts time.day    # => Day of date (1 to 31 )
puts time.wday # => 0: Day of week: 0 is Sunday
puts time.yday # => 365: Day of the year
puts time.hour # => 23: 24-hour clock
puts time.min    # => 59
puts time.sec    # => 59
puts time.usec # => 999999: microseconds
puts time.zone # => "UTC": timezone name
```

In date, the following terms can use:

- Calendar date: A calendar date is a certain day in the year.

- Ordinal date: The ordinal date is a specific day of the calendar year.

- Week date: A week date is a day in the calendar that represents a week.

- Julian day number: Since noon (Greenwich Mean Time) on January 1, 4713 BCE, the Julian day number has been in passed day (in the Julian calendar).

- Modified Julian day number: The Julian day number has been changed since midnight (Coordinated Universal Time) on November 17, 1858 CE (in the Gregorian calendar).

Example:

```
# program to illustrate different methods of date

# require 'date' is use to print the date on
screen
require 'date'

# print the Julian day number
puts Date.jd(2451377)

# print the commercial date
puts Date.commercial(2019,5,2)
puts Time.new(2019,4,6).to_date
puts Date.strptime('07-08-2018', '%d-%m-%Y')
```

```
# print the ordinal date
puts Date.ordinal(2018,15)
puts Date.new(2018,4,5)
```

DATE AND TIME DIRECTIVES

The strftime method employs the following directives:

- %a: The shortened term for a weekday (e.g., Sunday)

- %A: The weekday's full name (e.g., Sunday)

- %b: The month's abbreviated name (e.g., January)

- %B: The month's entire name (e.g., January)

- %c: The local date and time representation that was chosen

- %d: The month's day (1–31)

- %H: denotes a 24-h clock

- %I: 12-h clock

- %j: day of the year

- %m: month of the year

- %M: minute

- %p: meridian indicator

- %S: seconds

- %%: % literal

- %z: time zone name

- %Y: year name with century

- %y: year name without century

- %X: selected representation of the time only

- %x: selected representation of the date only

- %w: weekday

- %U: week number of current year, starting with first Sunday

- %W: week number of current year, starting with first Monday

Methods, recursion, hook methods, and range class methods were all discussed in this chapter. We also examined the initialize method, method overriding, date, and time.

NOTES

1. Ruby | Methods: https://www.geeksforgeeks.org/ruby-methods/, accessed on August 27, 2022.
2. Ruby – methods: https://www.tutorialspoint.com/ruby/ruby_methods.htm, accessed on August 27, 2022.
3. Method visibility in Ruby: https://www.geeksforgeeks.org/method-visibility-in-ruby/, accessed on August 28, 2022.
4. Ruby private and protected methods: understanding method visibility: https://www.rubyguides.com/2018/10/method-visibility/, accessed on August 27, 2022.
5. Recursion in Ruby: https://www.geeksforgeeks.org/recursion-in-ruby/, accessed on August 27, 2022.
6. Ruby hook methods: https://www.geeksforgeeks.org/ruby-hook-methods/, accessed on August 27, 2022.
7. Ruby | Range class methods: https://www.geeksforgeeks.org/ruby-range-class-methods/, accessed on August 29, 2022.
8. Range class methods in Ruby: https://www.tutorialspoint.com/range-class-methods-in-ruby, accessed on August 29, 2022.
9. The initialize method in Ruby: https://www.geeksforgeeks.org/the-initialize-method-in-ruby/, accessed on August 29, 2022.
10. Ruby | Method overriding: https://www.geeksforgeeks.org/ruby-method-overriding/, accessed on August 29, 2022.
11. Ruby method overriding: https://www.includehelp.com/ruby/method-overriding.aspx, accessed on August 29, 2022.
12. Ruby date and time: https://www.geeksforgeeks.org/ruby-date-and-time/, accessed on August 29, 2022.

## CHAPTER 6

Exceptions in Ruby

IN THIS CHAPTER

- ➢ Exceptions
- ➢ Exception Handling
- ➢ Catch and Throw Exception
- ➢ Raising Exceptions
- ➢ Exception Handling in Threads
- ➢ Exception Class and Its Method

In the previous chapter, we covered methods in Ruby, and in this chapter, we will discuss exceptions in Ruby.

A capable program (or programmer) arranges for faults and anticipates their occurrence. This is more complicated than it seems. Runtime errors are referred to as exceptions. It stops a program in its tracks. Many unexpected circumstances, such as running out of memory, being unable to open a file, attempting to initialize an object to an impossibly high number, and others, might cause them to occur.

WHAT EXACTLY IS AN EXCEPTION?

An exception is an unwanted or unexpected event that occurs as the code is being executed, or during runtime, and disrupts the orderly execution of the program's instructions.

Error versus Exception

Errors

- Errors are unforeseen issues that might arise when a computer program is being run.

- Errors are irreversible.

- The only exceptions are errors.

Exceptions

- Exceptions are unanticipated occurrences that may occur at run-time.

- Using try-catch techniques, exceptions may manage.

- Exceptions are not all mistakes.

Handling Exceptions in the Traditional Approach

Return codes are used in the conventional way of handling exceptions. The open method fails and returns a specified result. This value is then returned to the caller layer until someone needs to take responsibility for it. The issue with this technique was that handling all of these problems was extremely difficult.[1] If a method calls open, then read, and finally close, each call has the potential to provide an error signal. Now consider how the function will distinguish between these error codes in the value it returns to its caller.

The Exception class addresses this problem. The Exception class informs the application or programmer about an error that has occurred in an object. The exception object is returned to the caller stack until the system finds the appropriate code that knows how to address the problem.

The Exception Class and Its Hierarchy

It is the package that stores the exception data in an object. Ruby has a specified exception hierarchy.

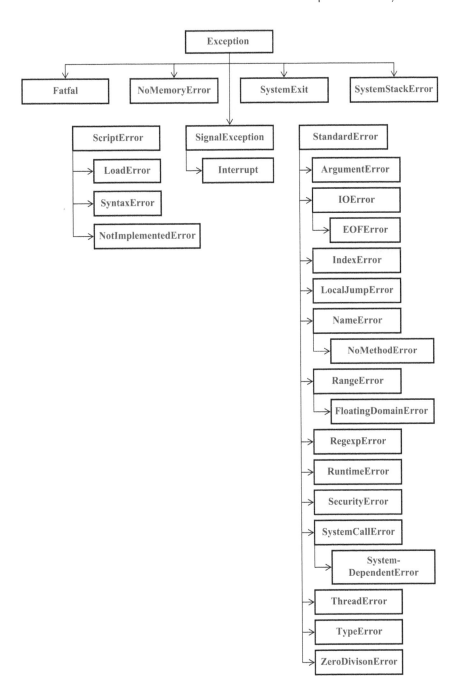

Hierarchy of Exception class.

In the above diagram, most exceptions fall under the StandardError class, representing generic errors that may occur in a Ruby program. The following exceptions indicate more dangerous, lower level, and less recoverable circumstances that are not handled by Ruby applications. A user can create an exception using one of the built-in exception classes. In Ruby, a user can also build their exception, but that exception must be a subclass of StandardError or one of its child classes. The exception would not be detected by default if he did not declare it in StandardError. Every exception has a message text as well as a stack retrace. So, if the user creates his exception, he must provide this data.

Example:

```
# program to illustrate the exception

# taking two integer value
$X = 22;
$Y = 0;

# divide by zero error
$Z = $X / $Y;

puts "Result is: #{$Z}"
```

Explanation: The user in the above software is attempting to divide 22 by 0. As a result, the Ruby compiler will raise a ZeroDivisionError exception.

Generating a User-Defined Exception

Ruby utilizes the kernel method raise to create exceptions that are instances of the Exception class or one of its subclasses. The rescue clause is used to manage raise exceptions.

Example:

```
# program to create the user defined exception

# define a method
def raise_exception

    puts 'This is Before the Exception Arise!'
```

```
    # using the raise to create exception
    raise 'Exception Create'

    puts 'This is After the Exception Arise -- Not
Displayed'
end

# Call the method
raise_exception
```

Solution to the preceding example code:

```
# program to create the user
# define the exception and rescued

# define a method
def raise_and_rescue
begin

    puts 'This is Before the Exception Arise!'

    # using the raise to create an exception
    raise 'Exception Create!'

    puts 'After the Exception'

# using the Rescue method
rescue
    puts 'Finally Saved!'

end

puts 'Outside from the Begin Block!'

end

# call method
raise_and_rescue
```

Explanation: In the preceding code, the exception is raised by the raise method (which comes straight from the kernel module), and the code is halted as a result of the presence of an exception. The rescue clause handles this exception, and the program flow continues without a problem following the rescue clause. If a code has more than one rescue clause, the following rescue clause will handle the exception if the previous rescue code cannot handle it.

EXCEPTION HANDLING IN RUBY

In Ruby, exception handling is a procedure that defines how to manage an error that occurs in a code. An error is defined in this context as an unwelcome or unexpected occurrence that occurs during the operation of a code, that is, during run time. It disturbs the usual flow of the program's instructions. As a result, the rescue block handled these sorts of failures. Ruby also has a distinct class for exceptions called an Exception class, which has several sorts of methods.[2]

Because the program in which an exception is generated is enclosed between the begin/end block, we may handle this form of exception with a rescue clause.

Syntax:

```
begin
    raise
      # block where the exception raise

    rescue
      # block where the exception rescue
end
```

Example:

```
# program to create the user
# define exception and handling it

# defie a method
def raise_and_rescue
begin

    puts 'This is Before the Exception Arise!'

    # using the raise to create an exception
    raise 'Exception Create!'
```

```
        puts 'After the Exception'

# using the Rescue method
rescue
        puts 'Finally Saved!'

end

puts 'Outside from the Begin Block!'

end

# call method
raise_and_rescue
```

Explanation: In the above code, an exception is raised in the begin block (raise block), interrupting the program's flow of the program. To get around this, utilize the rescue block to handle the raised exception. When a rescue block is utilized, it fixes the exception and resumes the program's performance.

Note that many rescue clauses can use in the same code, which implies that if the first rescue clause does not handle an exception, another rescue clause will. If no rescue clause matches, or if an exception arises outside the begin/end block, Ruby goes up the stack and searches the caller for an exception handler.

The following statements can be used in exceptions:

- **retry statement:** After catching the exception, this statement is used to restart the rescue block from the start.

    Syntax:

```
begin
        # block where the exception raise

rescue
        # block where exception is captured

retry

        # this statement restarts rescue
        # block from beginning
end
```

Example:

```
# program to illustrate
# use of the retry statement

begin

    # using the raise to create an exception
    raise 'Exception Created!'

    puts 'After the Exception'

# using the Rescue method
rescue
    puts 'Finally Saved!'

# using the retry statement
retry
end
```

Note: Take cautious when using the retry statement because it might lead to an infinite loop.

- **raise statement:** This statement causes an exception to be thrown.[3]

Syntax:

```
raise
```

This syntax is used to raise the current exception once again. It is often utilized by exception handlers when an exception is interrupted prior to being passed on.

```
raise "Error Message"
```

This syntax is being used to raise the call stack and cause a RuntimeError exception.

```
raise ExceptionType, "Error Message"
```

The first parameter in this syntax can use to cause an exception, and the second argument is used to set the message.

```
raise ExceptionType, "Error Message" condition
```

The first parameter in this syntax is used to cause an exception, and the second argument is used to set the message. A condition statement can also use to throw an exception.

Example:

```
# program to illustrate
# the use of raise statement

begin

    puts 'This is Before the Exception Arise!'

    # using the raise to create an exception
    raise 'Exception Create!'

    puts 'After the Exception'
end
```

- **ensure statement:** This line assures that necessary instructions are executed at the conclusion of the code, regardless of whether the exception raise or raised exception is rescued or the program ends due to an undetected exception. This block always outputs anything. This block is stacked on top of the rescue block.

Syntax:

```
begin
     # the exception raise

rescue
    # the exception rescue

ensure
    # this block always executes
end
```

Example:

```
# program to illustrate
# the use of ensure statement

begin
```

```
    # using the raise to create an exception
    raise 'Exception Created!'

    puts 'After the Exception'

# using the Rescue statement
rescue
    puts 'Finally Saved!'

# using the ensure statement
ensure
puts 'ensure block execute'
end
```

- **else statement:** This sentence appears between the rescue and assure blocks. This block is only executed only if no exception is thrown.

  Syntax:

```
begin
  rescue
    # the exception rescue

  else
    # this block executes when no exception is
raise

  ensure
    # this block always executes
end
```

  Example:

```
# program to illustrate
# the use of else statement

begin

    # using the raise to create an exception
    # raise 'Exception Created!'

    puts 'no Exception is raise'

    # using the Rescue method
```

```
    rescue
        puts 'Finally Saved!'

# using the else statement
else
        puts 'Else block execute because of no
exception is raise'

# using the ensure statement
ensure
    puts 'ensure block execute'
end
```

Catch and Throw in Exception Handling

In Ruby, catch and throw blocks are the lightweight method for error handling and are used to leap from the exception when no extra work is available in the code.

The catch block is used to leap out of the nested block, and the block is marked with a name. This block operates normally until it comes into contact with the toss block. The catch-and-toss approach will be faster than the lift-and-rescue method. When the throw statement is found, Ruby searches the call stack for the catch statement with the associated symbol. The throw statement never runs and always returns nil.

Syntax:

```
throw :label-name
    # this block will not execute

catch :label-name do
    # matching catch will execute when throw block
encounter
end
```

A condition may also be used in the catch and throw statement, as demonstrated below:

```
throw :label-name condition
    # this block will not execute

catch :label-name do
```

```
    # matching catch will execute when throw block
encounter
end
```

Example:

```
# program to illustrate
# the use of catch and throw statement

# define a method
def catch_and_throw(value)

puts value
m = readline.chomp

# using the throw statement
throw :value_e if m == "!"
return m

end

# using the catch statement
catch :value_e do

# enter the number
number = catch_and_throw("Enter Number: ")
end
```

Explanation: The catch and throw method is employed in the above code to output the value entered in the catch statement. If the user inputs a number, it will show the number, but if the user enters! , it will return nil because the throw statement was never ever performed.

CATCH AND THROW EXCEPTION IN RUBY

An exception is an instance of or a child of the class Exception. Exceptions arise when the program enters an undefined state during execution. Because the software is at a loss on what to do, it throws an exception. Ruby can accomplish this either automatically or manually. Exceptions may also be handled using the catch and throw keywords in Ruby, which are equivalent to the raise and rescue keywords.[4] When the throw keyword is used, an exception is generated, and program control is passed to the catch statement.

Syntax:

```
catch :lable-name do
# matching catch will execute when throw block
encounter

throw :lable-name condition
# this block will not execute

end
```

The catch block is used to exit the nested block, and it is marked with a name. This block functions normally until it comes into contact with the throw block, which is why catch and throw are used instead of raise or rescue.

First example:

```
# Program of Catch and Throw Exception
pfp = catch(:divide) do
# code block of the catch similar to begin
    number = rand(2)
    throw :divide if number == 0
    number # set pfp = number if
    # no exception is thrown
end
puts pfp
```

If the number is 0 in the above case, the exception:divide is thrown, which returns nothing to the catch statement, resulting in "" set to pfp. If the value is 1, no exception is thrown, and the pfp variable is set to 1.

Second example: When the exception was thrown in the preceding case, the value of variable pfp was set to "". We may adjust that by supplying the throw keyword the default argument.

```
# Program of Catch and Throw Exception
pfp = catch(:divide) do
# a code block of the catch similar to begin
    number = rand(2)
    throw :divide, 12 if number == 0
    number # set pfp = number if
    # no exception is thrown
end
puts pfp
```

Third example: A nested construct instance, in which we will show how to exit nested constructs.

```
# Program of Catch and Throw Exception
pfp = catch(:divide) do
# a code block of the catch similar to begin
    120.times do
    120.times do
        120.times do
        number = rand(12000)
        # comes out of all of loops
        # and goes to catch statement
        throw :divide, 12 if number == 0
        end
    end
    end
    number # set pfp = number if
    # no exception is thrown
end
puts pfp
```

RAISING EXCEPTIONS IN RUBY

An exception is an undesired or unexpected occurrence that occurs during program execution, that is, at runtime, and disturbs the usual flow of the program's instructions. As we understand, the code enclosed within the begin-and-end blocks is completely secure for handling exceptions, and the rescue block informs Ruby about the sort of exception to be treated.[5]

Specifically, runtime exceptions are handled if there is a mistake in the code, maybe authored by an inexperienced developer; these sorts of errors may include "division by zero error," "index out of range error," and so on, and the program will cease executing if these exceptions are not handled. We may manually raise user-defined exceptions by using the raise statement. For example, in an ATM transaction software, an exception is raised when a user inputs an incorrect account number to withdraw.

Syntax:

```
raise exception-type "exception message" condition
```

When the raise statement is elevated, the rescue is called, and the execution begins. By default, the raise command throws a RuntimeError.

Example:

```
# program to illustrate
# the use of raise statement

begin

    puts 'This is Before the Exception Arise!'

    # using the raise to create an exception
    raise 'Exception Create!'

    puts 'After the Exception'
end
```

- Check out the four different sorts of raise commands in the code below:

```
#!/usr/bin/ruby
puts "type-1\n"
begin

# re-raises current exception
# (RuntimeError as they are no current exception)
raise
rescue
puts 'Rony got rescued.'
end
puts 'Rony returned safely'

puts "\ntype-2\n"
begin

# sets this message to the string in superclass,
# this exception will given top priority in call
stack.
raise 'Quill got rescued.'
puts 'quill' # won't execute
rescue StandardError => e
puts e.message
end
puts 'The Quill is back to ship.'
```

```
puts "\ntype-3\n"
begin
# uses first argument to create an exception
# and then sets message to the second argument.
raise StandardError.new 'Groot got rescued.'
rescue StandardError => e # e=>object

# prints attached string message.
puts e.message
end

puts "\ntype-4\n"
begin
a = 30
b = 0
# here conditional statement is added
# to execute only if statement is true

    # raises exception only if condition is true
    raise ZeroDivisionError.new 'b should not be
0' if b == 0
    puts a/b
rescue StandardError => e
puts e.message
end

puts
begin
a = 30

# changing b value, it passes raise and executes
further
b = 2

    # raises the exception only if condition is
true
    raise ZeroDivisionError.new 'b should not be
0' if b == 0
    print "a/b = ", a / b
rescue StandardError => e
puts e.message
end
```

- Examine the distinction between Runtime and Raised Exception.

Example:

```
#!/usr/bin/ruby
puts "the Raised Exception:\n"
begin
a = 30
b = 0

    # raises exception only if condition is true
    raise ZeroDivisionError.new 'b should not be
0' if b == 0
    print "a/b = ", (1 + 2) * (a / b)
rescue ZeroDivisionError => e
puts e.message

# prints error stack, but a raised exception has
zero stack
puts e.backtrace
end

puts "\nRuntime Exception:\n"
begin
a = 30
b = 0
x=(1 + 2) * (a / b)

    # raises exception only if condition is true
    raise ZeroDivisionError.new 'b should not 0'
if b == 0
    print "a/b = ", (1 + 2) * (a / b)
rescue ZeroDivisionError => e

# prints message=>(divided by 0)
# from ZeroDivisionError class
puts e.message
puts e.backtrace
end
```

- In the above instance, Runtime Exception contains an error stack.

EXCEPTION HANDLING IN THREADS IN RUBY

Exceptions can also be seen in threads. In Ruby threads, the only exception that occurs in the main thread is handled, but if an exception occurs in the thread (other than the main thread), the thread is terminated.[6] The occurrence of an exception in a thread other than the main thread is determined by the abort_on_exception method. The value of abort_on_exception is set to false by default. When the value of abort_on_exception is false, it signifies that the unhandled exception terminates the current thread but leaves the other threads running.

We may also adjust the abort_on_exception option by using abort_on_exception=true or setting $DEBUG to true. Ruby threads additionally provide a method for dealing with exceptions, namely, ::handle_interrupt. This function will deal with exceptions asynchronously.

Example:

```
# program to illustrate
# exception in thread

#!/usr/bin/ruby

threads = []
4.times do |value|

    threads << Thread.new(value) do |m|

        # raising an error when m become 2
        raise "oops error!" if m == 2

print "#{m}\n"
end

end
threads.each {|n| n.join }
```

The Thread.Join function is used to wait for a certain thread to complete. Because when a Ruby application stops, all threads are destroyed regardless of status. We may also store the exception, as seen in the code below:

```
# program to illustrate how to
# escape exception
```

```
#!/usr/bin/ruby

threads = []

5.times do |value|
    threads << Thread.new(value) do |m|
        raise "oops error!" if m == 3
print "#{m}\n"
end

end

threads.each do |n|
begin

n.join

# using the rescue method
rescue RuntimeError => o
    puts "Failed:: #{o.message}"
end
end
```

Set abort_on_exception to true to kill the thread that includes an exception. No additional output will be produced once the thread has died.

Example:

```
# program to illustrate the killing
# of thread in which the exception raised

#!/usr/bin/ruby

# setting value of abort_on_exception
Thread.abort_on_exception = true

threads = []

5.times do |value|
    threads << Thread.new(value) do |m|
    raise "oops error!" if m == 3
```

```
print "#{m}\n"
end

end


# using the Thread.Join Method
threads.each {|n| n.join }
```

EXCEPTION CLASS AND ITS METHODS IN RUBY

An exception is an unwelcome or unexpected occurrence that happens during the execution of a program, that is, at runtime, and disturbs the usual flow of the program's instructions. Exception descendants are used in Ruby to interface between raise methods and rescue statements in begin-and-end blocks.[7]

Exception objects include data about the exception, such as its type, a descriptive text, and optional data.

Methods for Exception Classes

- **exception:** This function produces and returns a new exception object.

  ```
  Exception.exception(message)
  ```

- **new:** This method generates a new exception object and returns it, optionally setting message to message.

  ```
  Exception.new(message)
  ```

  Example:

  ```
  # program to illustrate
  # the use of new method

  # create the customized class
  # inherited from the StandardError
  class MyException < StandardError
  attr_reader :myobject

  def initialize(myobject)
      @myobject = myobject
  end
  end

  begin
  ```

```
# Using the new method
# to create an object of the
# given exception
raise MyException.new("My object"), "This is the
custome class"
rescue MyException => e
puts e.message
puts e.myobject
end
```

- **backtrace:** This function retrieves any backtrace information associated with exc. The backtrace is an array of strings that includes either the filename:line:in method or the filename:line method.

```
exc.backtrace
```

Example:

```
# program to illustrate
# the use of backtrace method

# define method
def a1

# raise the exception
raise "OOPs! The exception raise"
end

# define method
def a2
# call method a1
a1()
end

begin
# call method a2
a2()
# rescue the exception
rescue => a_Details

# print backtrace details
# related with the exception
puts a_Details.backtrace.join("\n")
end
```

- **exception:** Return the receiver if there is no argument or if the argument is the same as the receiver. Otherwise, make a new exception object of the same class as the receiver with the message string.to_str.

```
exc.exception(message)
```

- **message:** This method returns a message relating to exc.

```
exc.message
```

- **set_backtrace:** This function configures the backtrace data for exc. This must take an array of string objects in the format provided in Exception#backtrace as an input.

```
exc.set_backtrace(array)
```

- **to_s:** This function returns the message associated with exc or the name of the exception if no message is specified.

```
exc.to_s
```

Example:

```
# program to illustrate
# the use of to_s method

begin

# raise the exception
raise "Ruby Exception"

# rescue the exception
rescue Exception => a

# print the message
puts a.to_s
end
```

- **inspect:** This method returns the class name and message of the exception.

```
exc.inspect
```

- **cause:** This method returns the prior exception that occurred when exc was raised.

- ==: This method returns true if the object and exc have the same class, message, and backtrace. If not, it returns false.

In this chapter, we discussed what an exception is, how to handle exceptions, and how to catch and throw exceptions. We also discussed raising exceptions, exception handling in threads, and the exception class and its method.

NOTES

1. Ruby | Exceptions: https://www.geeksforgeeks.org/ruby-exceptions/, accessed on August 29, 2022.
2. Ruby | Exception handling: https://www.geeksforgeeks.org/ruby-exception-handling/, accessed on August 29, 2022.
3. Exception handling in Ruby: https://scoutapm.com/blog/exception-handling-in-ruby, accessed on August 29, 2022.
4. Catch and throw exception in Ruby: https://www.geeksforgeeks.org/catch-and-throw-exception-in-ruby/, accessed on August 30, 2022.
5. Raising exceptions in Ruby: https://www.geeksforgeeks.org/raising-exceptions-in-ruby/, accessed on August 30, 2022.
6. Ruby | Exception handling in threads | Set 1: https://www.geeksforgeeks.org/ruby-exception-handling-in-threads-set-1/, accessed on August 30, 2022.
7. Ruby | Exception class and its methods: https://www.geeksforgeeks.org/ruby-exception-class-and-its-methods/, accessed on August 30, 2022.

## CHAPTER 7

Regex and Classes in Ruby

IN THIS CHAPTER

➤ Regular Expressions

➤ Search and Replace

➤ Different Types of Classes in Ruby(Float, integer, Symbol, Struct)

➤ Dir Class and Its Methods

➤ MatchData Class

In the previous chapter, we covered exceptions in Ruby, and in this chapter, we will discuss regex and classes in Ruby.

REGULAR EXPRESSIONS IN RUBY

A regular expression is a string of characters that defines a search pattern. It is commonly used in string pattern matching. Ruby regular expressions, or Ruby regex for short, allow us to discover specific patterns inside a text.[1] Validation and parsing are two applications of ruby regex. Ruby regex may use to validate email addresses as well as IP addresses. Ruby regex expressions are declared by separating them with two forward slashes.

DOI: 10.1201/9781003358510-7

Syntax:

```
# find the word 'hi'
"Hey there, i am using pfp" =~ /hey/
```

This will provide the index of the first occurrence of the word "hey" if it exists, otherwise it will return "nil."

Checking Whether a String Includes a Regex

Using the match method, we can also determine whether or not a text contains a regex. Here's an example to help us understand.

Example:

```
# program of regular expression

# Checking if word is present in the string
if "hey there".match(/hey/)
    puts "match"
end
```

Checking Whether a String Contains a Specific Set of Characters

We may use a character class to provide a set of characters for the match. For instance, if we wish to find a vowel, we may use the match [aeiou].[2]

Example:

```
# program of regular expression

# declare a function that checks for the vowel in
a string
def contains_vowel(str)
str =~ /[aeiou]/
end

# the Driver code

# Peeks has vowel at index 1, so the function
returns 1
puts( contains_vowel("Peeks") )

# bcd has no vowel, so return nil and nothing is
printed
puts( contains_vowel("bcd") )
```

Various Regular Expressions

Character ranges can be specified using several short expressions:

- \w is the same as [0-9a-zA-Z_].

- [0-9] is the same as\d.

- \s corresponds to white space.

- \W anything that isn't in [0-9a-zA-Z_].

- \D everything that isn't a number.

- \S anything other than a space.

- The character of the dot matches everything except the new line. If we wish to seek for character, we must first escape it.

Example:

```
# program of regular expression

a="2m3"
b="2.5"
# . literal matches for all the character
if(a.match(/\d.\d/))
    puts("match is found")
else
    puts("not found")
end
# after escaping it, it matches with only '.'
literal
if(a.match(/\d\.\d/))
    puts("match is found")
else
    puts("not found")
end

if(b.match(/\d.\d/))
    puts("match is found")
else
    puts("not found")
end
```

Regexp Modifiers

We may use modifiers to match several characters:

- + represents one or more characters.
- indicates that there are 0 or more characters.
- ? denotes a 0 or 1 character.
- {x, y} if the number of characters between x and y is between x and y.
- When matching text, i is for ignoring case.
- In regular expressions, x is for ignores whitespace and permits comments.
- m stands for multiple-line matches, and newlines are treated as regular characters.
- The characters u,e,s,n are used to interpret the regexp as Unicode (UTF-8), EUC, SJIS, or ASCII. If none of these modifiers are supplied, the regular expression is considered to utilize the source encoding.

SEARCH AND REPLACE IN RUBY

Regular expression string techniques sub and gsub, as well as in-place versions sub! and gsub! The sub & sub! substitutes the pattern's initial occurrence, whereas gsub & gsub! replaces all instances. All of these approaches use a Regexp pattern to accomplish a search-and-replace operation.[3] The sub! and gsub! functions modify the string on which they are called, whereas the sub and gsub functions return a new string while keeping the original unchanged.

Here's an example to help us understand it better.

```
# program of sub and gsub method in string

roll = "2004-959-559 # This is the Roll Number"

# Delete the Ruby-style comments
roll = roll.sub!(/#.*$/, "")
puts "Roll Num is: #{roll}"

# Remove anything other than digits
roll = roll.gsub!(/\D/, "")
puts "Roll Num is: #{roll}"
```

Sub! and gsub! are used in the preceding example. In this case, sub! replaces the first occurrence of the pattern, but gsub! replaces all instances.

```
# program of sub and gsub method
text = "peeks for peeks, is a computer science portal"

# Change "rails" to "Rails" throughout
text.gsub!("peeks", "Peeks")

# Capitalize word "Rails" throughout
text.gsub!(/\bpeeks\b/, "Peeks")
puts "#{text}"
```

The gsub! technique can also be used with a regular expression.

FLOAT CLASS IN RUBY

In Ruby, the Float class is a subclass of the Numeric class. The Float class objects understand actual numbers using the native architecture's double-precision floating-point interpretation.[4]

Methods for Creating Public Instances

1. **Arithmetic operations:** Several arithmetic operations on float are performed by this approach.

   • **Addition:** It gives the sum of a float and a set of numbers as a floating-point number.

   ```
   float + numeric
   ```

   • **Subtraction:** It returns the difference between a float and a numeric value as a floating-point number.

   ```
   float - numeric
   ```

   • **Multiplication:** It returns the product of a float and a numeric value in the form of a floating-point number.

   ```
   float * numeric
   ```

   • **Division:** It returns the result of dividing a float by a numeric value in a floating-point number.

   ```
   float / numeric
   ```

- **Modulo:** This function returns the modulo of a float and a numeric value in floating-point numbers.

```
float % numeric
```

- **Exponent:** It returns the product of the float's power and the numeric value in floating-point numbers.

```
float ** numeric
```

- **Unary minus:** The unary minus function returns a floating-point value.

```
float -@
```

Example:

```
# program to illustrate
# the Arithmetic operation

m = 3.1
n = 3

# Addition
o = m + n

puts "addition #{o}"

# Subtraction
p = m - n

puts "subtraction #{p}"

# Multiplication
q = m * n

puts "multiplication #{q}"

# Division
r = m / n

puts "division #{r}"

# Modulo
s = m % n
```

```
      puts "modulo #{s}"

      # Exponent
      t = m ** n

      puts "exponent #{t}"

      # Unary minus
      u= -m

      puts "unary minus #{u}"
```

2. <=>: Depending on the float, this method returns −1, 0, or +1. If float is less than numeric value, it returns −1; if float is equal to numeric value, it returns 0, and if float is more than numeric value, it returns +1.

```
float <=> numeric --> 1, 0, +1
```

Example:

```
# program to illustrate
# the <=> Method

puts 2.1 <=> 4
puts 2.0 <=> 2
puts 4.6 <=> 2
```

3. ==: If the obj is equal to float, this method returns true; else, it returns false.

```
float == obj --> true or false
```

Example:

```
# program to illustrate
# the == Method

puts 3.8 == 4
puts 3.8 == 3.8
```

4. **abs:** This method returns the float's absolute value.

```
float.abs --> numeric
```

Example:

```
# program to illustrate
# the abs Method
```

```
puts (-54.56).abs
puts (-65.04).abs
```

5. **ceil:** Returns the smallest Integer that is greater than or equal to float. This method's return type is int.

```
float.ceil --> int
```

Example:

```
# program to illustrate
# the ceil Method

puts (4.1).ceil
puts (4.0).ceil
puts (-4.1).ceil
```

6. **divmod:** Returns an array containing the quotient and modulus obtained by dividing num by numeric.

```
float.divmod(numeric) --> array
```

Example:

```
# program to illustrate
# the divmod Method

p (45.0.divmod 5)
p (98.0.divmod 5)
```

7. **eql?:** This method determines whether the obj is a Float with the same value as in float. If they have the same value, it will return true; otherwise, it will return false. This method's return type is Boolean.[5]

```
float.eql?(obj) --> true or false
```

Example:

```
# program to illustrate
# the eql? Method

puts 4.2.eql?(2)
puts 1.2.eql?(1.2)
```

8. **finite?:** This technique determines whether the float is an IEEE floating-point number. If float is a valid IEEE floating-point number, it returns true; otherwise, it returns false.

```
float.finite? --> true or false
```

Example:

```
# program to illustrate
# the finite? Method

puts (46.0).finite?
puts (46.0/0.0).finite?
```

9. **floor:** This function returns the greatest integer that is less than or equal to float.

```
float.floor --> int
```

Example:

```
# program to illustrate
# the floor Method

puts 2.2. floor
puts (-4.6).floor
```

10. **infinite?:** This method returns nil, −1, or +1 depending on the value of float. If float is finite, it returns nil, if it is infinite, it returns −1, and if it is +infinite, it returns +1.

```
float.infinite? --> nil, -1, +1
```

Example:

```
# program to illustrate
# the infinite? Method

puts (1.1).infinite?
puts (-1.1/0.0).infinite?
puts (+1.1/0.0).infinite?
```

11. **modulo:** This technique is identical to the Float#% method.

```
float.modulo(numeric) --> numeric
```

Example:

```
# program to illustrate
# the modulo Method

puts 32.45.modulo(20)
```

12. **nan?:** If float is an incorrect IEEE floating-point number, this method returns true; else, it returns false. This method's return type is Boolean.

```
float.nan? --> true or false
```

Example:

```
# program to illustrate
# the nan? Method

puts (-2.2). nan?
puts (0.0/0.0). nan?
```

13. **round:** Rounds a float value to the nearest integer value. This method's return type is int.

```
float..round(digits=0) --> numeric
```

Example:

```
# Ruby program to illustrate
# round Method

puts 6.7.round
puts (-8.9).round
```

14. **to_f:** This function returns a float.

```
float.to_f --> float
```

15. **to_i:** This function returns a float that has been truncated to an integer. This method's return type is int.

```
float.to_i --> int
```

Example:

```
# program to illustrate
# the to_i Method

puts 5.6.to_i
```

16. **to_int:** This function is analogous to Float#to_i.

```
float.to_int --> int
```

17. **to_s:** This function provides a string including a self-representation and a fixed or exponential numbering scheme. The function may return NaN, infinity, or −infinity.

```
float.to_s --> string
```

18. **truncate:** This technique is equivalent to the Float#to_i method. This method's return type is int.

```
float.truncate
```

19. **zero?:** If float is 0.0, this function returns true; otherwise, it returns false. This method's return type is Boolean.

```
float.zero? --> true or false
```

Example:

```
# program to illustrate
# the zero? Method

puts (0.0).zero?
puts (1.4).zero?
```

The Float class include the following constants:

Constants	Description
DIG	It stores the minimum number of useful decimal digits in a double-precision floating point, which is 15 by default.
EPSILON	It defaults to 2.2204460492503131e−16 and contains the difference between 1 and the lowest double-precision floating point value higher than 1.
MANT_DIG	It stores the number of RADIX mantissa digits. The default value is 53.
MAX	It stores the biggest feasible integer in a double-precision floating point number, which is 1.7976931348623157e+308.
MAX_10_EXP	It is the biggest positive exponent in a double-precision floating point when 10 is increased to this power minus one. 308 is the default value.
MAX_EXP	It is the maximum allowable exponent value in a double-precision floating point, which is 1024 by default.
MIN	In a double-precision floating point, it is the lowest positive normalized number. The default value is 2.2250738585072014e−308.
MIN_10_EXP	In a double-precision floating point, it is the smallest negative exponent where 10 is increased to this power minus 1. −307 is the default value.

(Continued)

Constants	Description
MIN_EXP	In a double-precision floating point, it is the lowest possible exponent value. −1021 is the default value.
RADIX	The radix of floating-point representations, or the basis of floating-point numbers. Most systems have a default value of 2, representing a base 10 decimal.
ROUND	It is the manner of rounding for floating-point operations. The values are as follows: −1: If the mode is undetermined, the value is −1. 0: If rounding to the nearest integer. If the rounding is closest to a representable value, the value is 1. 2: If the rounding is in the direction of +infinite. 3: If the rounding is in the direction of +infinite.
NaN	It represents a value that is "not a number."
INFINITY	It is an expression for positive infinity.

INTEGER CLASS IN RUBY

The Integer class in Ruby serves as the foundation for the two concrete classes that contain whole numbers. Bignum and Fixnum are the concrete classes. Fixnum stores integer values that are displayed in the native machine word, whereas Bignum stores integer values that are outside of Fixnum's range.[6] The Integer class includes a diverse set of methods for carrying out certain tasks. The Numeric class is a subclass of the Integer class.

The following are the methods defined under the integer class:

- to_i
- downto
- chr
- floor
- integer?
- times
- upto
- next
- ceil

- to_int

- truncate

- round

- succ

1. **to_i:** This method returns an int value. This method's synonym is to_int.

   Syntax:

   ```
   int.to_i
   ```

2. **chr:** This method returns a string containing the ASCII character represented by the value of the receiver. This method's return type is string.

   Syntax:

   ```
   int.char
   ```

   Example:

   ```
   # program for explaining
   # the chr method

   puts 65.chr
   puts? a.chr
   ```

3. **downto:** This technique is used in the iterator block to transfer decreasing values from int down to and including the integer. This method's return type is an integer.

   Syntax:

   ```
   int.downto(integer){|x| block}
   ```

   Example:

   ```
   # program for explaining
   # the downto method

   6.downto(1){|i| print i, "..."}
   print "stop"
   ```

4. **floor:** The biggest integer less than or equal to int is returned by this procedure. This technique is the same as the to_i method. This method's return type is integer.

Syntax:

```
int.floor
```

Example:

```
# program for explaining
# the floor method

puts 1.floor
puts (-1).floor
```

5. **integer?:** This function always returns true when the value is an integer and false when it is not. This method's return type is Boolean.

Syntax:

```
int.integer?
```

Example:

```
# program for explaining
# the integer? method

puts 2.integer?
puts 0.1.integer?
```

6. **next:** This function returns the integer corresponding to int+1. This method's return type is an integer. succ is a synonym for this procedure.[7]

Syntax:

```
int.next
int.succ
```

Example:

```
# program for explaining
# the next method

puts 5.next
puts -20.next
```

7. **times:** This function iterates block int times, passing in values ranging from zero to int-1. This method's return type is integer.

Syntax:

```
int.times{|i| block}
```

Example:

```
# program for explaining
# the times method

6.times do|i|
print i, " "
end
```

8. **upto:** This method iterates block, handing in integer values ranging from int to and including the value of the receiver. This method's return type is integer.

Syntax:

```
int.upto(integer){|i| block}
```

Example:

```
# program for explaining
# the upto method

20.upto(25){|a| print a, "... "}
```

9. **round:** This function rounds the integer value. When the provided value is positive, it returns a floating-point number, self when it is zero, and rounded down when it is negative.

Syntax:

```
int.round
```

Example:

```
# program for explaining
# the round method

puts 2.round
puts (29.67).round
```

SYMBOL CLASS IN RUBY

The Symbol class objects represent the names found within the Ruby interpreter. They are often created using : name literal syntax or to_sym techniques. Symbol objects of a similar kind are produced for a given name string for the length of a program's implementation, irrespective of the name's content or meaning.[8]

Example:

```
# program to illustrate
# the Symbol objects

# context 3
module Peeks1

class Max
end
$m1 = :Max
end

# context 1
module Peeks2

Max = 1
$m2 = :Max
end

# context 2
def Max()

end

$m3 = :Max

puts $m1.object_id
puts $m2.object_id
puts $m3.object_id
```

Class Method

all_symbols: This function returns an array of Ruby symbols that are presently in the symbol table.

```
Symbol.all_symbols
```

Example:

```
# program to illustrate the
# use of all_symbol method

# Using the all_symbol method
puts Symbol.all_symbols.size
puts Symbol.all_symbols[1, 22]
```

Instance Methods

1. **id2name:** This function returns a string representing sym.

   ```
   sym.id2name
   ```

   Example:

   ```
   # program to illustrate the
   # use of id2name method

   # Using the id2name method
   p :Peeks.id2name
   p :"Welcome to PeeksforPeeks Portal".id2name
   ```

2. **inspect:** This function returns the symbol literal representation of sym.

   ```
   sym.inspect
   ```

   Example:

   ```
   # program to illustrate the
   # use of inspect method

   # Using the inspect method
   p :peeks.inspect
   p :"welcome to peeksforpeeks portal".inspect
   ```

3. **to_s:** This function is identical to Symbol#id2name. This function returns the name or a string representing sym.

   ```
   sym.to_s
   ```

   Example:

   ```
   # program to illustrate the
   # use of to_s method
   ```

```
# Using the to_s method
p :peeks.to_s
p :"welcome to peeksforpeeks portal".to_s
```

4. <=>: After calling to_s, it compares sym to other_sym. It returns −1 if sym is less than other_sym, 0 if sym equals other_sym, and +1 if sym is greater than other_sym.

```
sym <=> other_sym
```

Example:

```
# program to illustrate
# the use of <=>

# Using the <=>
a= :peeks
b = :"welcome to peeksforpeeks portal"
puts a<=>b
c= :peeks
puts a<=>c
puts b<=>a
```

5. ==: If the sym is equal to the obj, it returns true; otherwise, it returns false.

```
sym== obj
```

Example:

```
# program to illustrate
# use of the ==

# Using the ==
a= :peeks
b = :"welcome to peeksforpeeks portal"
puts a==b
c= :peeks
puts a==c
```

6. []: This method returns the sym.to_s[] value.

```
sym[idx]   --> char
sym[b, n]  --> string
```

7. **capitalize:** This technique is comparable to Symbol#to_s.

```
sym.capitalize
```

8. **casecmp:** A case-insensitive version of the symbol <=$gt;. It will return a value of −1, 0, 1, or nil. It only works on A–Z/a–z, not entire Unicode. When the two symbols have incompatible encodings or other_sym is not a symbol, this function returns nil.

```
sym.casecmp(other)
```

Example:

```
# program to illustrate
# the use of casecmp method

# Using casecmp method
puts :PeeKs.casecmp(:peeks)
puts :PeeKsPfp.casecmp(:peeksP)
puts :PeeKsPfp.casecmp(:peeksPfpz)
puts :PeeKsPfp.casecmp(3)
```

9. **downcase:** This approach changes uppercase letters to lowercase letters.

```
sym.downcase
```

Example:

```
# program to illustrate
# the use of the downcase method

# Using downcase method
puts :"WELCOME TO PEEKSFORPEEKS".downcase
```

10. **length:** The length of the specified sym is returned by this procedure.

```
sym.length
```

Example:

```
# program to illustrate
# the use of length method

# Using the length method
puts :PeeKsPfp.length
```

11. **slice:** Symbol#to_s is identical to this method. This function returns the character at the specified index from the sym.

```
sym.slice(index)
sym.slice(b, n)
```

Example:

```
# program to illustrate
# the use of slice method

# Using the slice method
p :PeeKsPfp.slice(3)
p :PeeKsPfp.slice(6)
```

12. **swapcase:** This method switches the case of the characters in sym. In other words, it transforms lowercase letters to uppercase letters and uppercase letters to lowercase letters.

```
sym.swapcase
```

Example:

```
# program to illustrate
# the use of the swapcase method

# Using the swapcase method
p "WELcome TO peeksFORPEEKS".swapcase
```

13. **upcase:** Converts lowercase characters to uppercase characters.

```
sym.upcase
```

Example:

```
# program to illustrate
# the use of the upcase method

# Using the upcase method
p "welcome to peeksforpeeks".upcase
```

14. **to_proc:** This function returns a Proc object that responds to the method specified by sym.

```
sym.to_proc
```

Example:

```
# program to illustrate
# the use of to_proc method

# Using the to_proc method
p (1..5).collect(&:to_s)
```

15. **to_sym:** This function returns a symbol representing an item. Because sym was already a symbol in this situation, it returns it.

```
sym.to_sym
```

STRUCT CLASS IN RUBY

Struct is a concise technique to use accessor methods to gather together a number of characteristics without establishing an explicit class.[9] The Struct class creates other classes, each of which is specified to store a collection of variables and associated accessors. Struct::Tms is a subclass of Struct.

Example:

```
# program to illustrate
# the use of Struct

# create Struct
# Peek is generated class
Peek = Struct.new(:tut_name, :cate_name) do

def pfp

    "This is the #{cate_name} class tutorial in
#{tut_name}."

end
end

# create object of struct
a = Peek.new("Ruby", "Struct")
puts a.pfp
```

Class Method

new: This function generates a new class named string that has accessor methods for the specified symbols. The anonymous structure class is constructed if the name string is not specified. Otherwise, the name of this struct will use as a constant in the Struct class; therefore, it must be unique among all Structs in the system and begin with capital letters. When a structured class is assigned to a constant, the class is essentially given the constant's name.

```
Struct.new([string] [, symbol])
Struct.new([string] [, symbol]){block}
```

Example:

```
# program to illustrate
# create the structure

# Create structure with a name in struct
Struct.new("Peek", :tutorial_name, :topic_name)
Struct::Peek.new("ruby", "Struct")

# Create structure named by its constant
Peek = Struct.new(:tutorial_name, :topic_name)
p Peek.new("Ruby", "Struct")
```

Struct.new returns a new class object that may use to build a specific instance of the new structure. The actual parameter in this case is fewer than or equal to the number of attributes provided for this class. Unset parameters have a default value of nil. An ArgumentError exception will be thrown if too many parameters are provided.

```
Peek.new([obj])
```

Example:

```
# program to illustrate
# create the objects of structure

# Create the structure
Peek = Struct.new(:tutorial_name, :topic_name)

# Create the objects
str = Peek.new("Ruby", "Struct")
p str.tutorial_name
p str.topic_name
```

Instance Method

1. ==: Equality is the term for this. It returns true if str and other_struct have the same example variable values. They must also be of the same class as the one produced by Struct.new. If not, it returns false.

   ```
   str == other_struct
   ```

Example:

```
# program to illustrate
# check the equality

# Create the structure
Peek = Struct.new(:tutorial_name, :topic_name)

# Create the objects
str = Peek.new("Ruby", "Struct")
other_struct = Peek.new("Java", "array")
str1 = Peek.new("Ruby", "Struct")

# Check the equality
p str == other_struct
p str == str1
```

2. []: This is referred to as Attribute Reference. It returns the instance variable named by symbol or index(0..length-1) by int. If the named variable does not exist, NameError is raised, and if the index is out of range, IndexError is raised.

```
str[symbol]
str[int]
```

Example:

```
# program to illustrate
# the use of []

# Create the structure
Peek = Struct.new(:tutorial_name, :topic_name)

# Create the objects
str = Peek.new("Ruby", "Struct")

# Using the []
p str[:tutorial_name]
p str["topic_name"]
```

3. []=: It's called Parameter Assignment. It is employed to return the int value of obj or the symbol name of the instance variable. If the instance variable's name does not exist or the index is out of range, it throws a NameError.

```
str[symbol] = obj
str[int] = obj
```

Example:

```
# program to illustrate
# the use of []=

# Create the structure
Peek = Struct.new(:tutorial_name, :topic_name)

# Create the objects
str = Peek.new("Ruby", "Struct")

# Using the []=
str[:tutorial_name]= "Java"
str[:topic_name]= "array"
p str.tutorial_name
p str.topic_name
```

4. **each:** For each instance variable, this method calls block and passes the value as an argument.

```
str.each_pair{|obj| block}
```

Example:

```
# program to illustrate
# the use of each method

# Create the structure
Peek = Struct.new(:tutorial_name, :topic_name)

# Create the objects
str = Peek.new("Ruby", "Struct")

# Using the each method
str.each{|a| puts (a)}
```

5. **each_pair:** For each instance variable, this method runs block and passes the name and value as parameters.

```
str.each_pair{|symbol, obj| block}
```

Example:

```
# program to illustrate
# the use of each_pair method
```

```
# Create the structure
Peek = Struct.new(:tutorial_name, :topic_name)

# Create the objects
str = Peek.new("Ruby", "Struct")

# Using the each_pair method
str.each_pair{|tutorial_name, a| puts
("#{tutorial_name} => #{a}")}
```

6. **length:** The number of instance variables returned by this function. This method's return type is an integer.

```
str.length
```

Example:

```
# program to illustrate
# the use of length method

# Create the structure
Peek = Struct.new(:tutorial_name, :topic_name)

# Create the objects
str = Peek.new("Ruby", "Struct")

# Using length method
p str.length
```

7. **members:** This function returns a string array containing the name of the instance variable.

```
str.members
```

Example:

```
# program to illustrate
# the use of members

# Create the structure
Peek = Struct.new(:tutorial_name, :topic_name)

# Create the objects
str = Peek.new("Ruby", "Struct")

# Using the members method
p str.members
```

8. **size:** size is identical to the Struct#length function. This method's return type is an integer.

```
str.size
```

9. **to_a:** This function returns an array of the values for this instance.

```
str.to_a
```

Example:

```
# program to illustrate
# the use of to_a method

# Create the structure
Peek = Struct.new(:tutorial_name, :topic_name)

# Creating objects
str = Peek.new("Ruby", "Struct")

# Using the to_a method
p str.to_a[0]
p str.to_a[1]
```

10. **values:** This technique is comparable to the Struct#to_a method.

```
str.values
```

11. **values_at:** This function returns an array containing the str elements corresponding to the provided indices. Integer indices or ranges can be used as selectors.

```
str.values_at([selector])
```

Example:

```
# program to illustrate
# the use of value_at method

# Create the structure
Peek = Struct.new(:p, :q, :r, :s)

# Create the objects
str = peek.new(15, 16, 17, 18)

# Using the values_at method
p str.values_at(2, 1)
p str.values_at(2, 1, 0, 3)
```

DIR CLASS AND ITS METHODS IN RUBY

A directory is a storage location for files. The Dir class in Ruby manages directories, while the File class manages files. In directories, a double dot (..) represents the parent directory while a single dot (.) represents the directory itself.[10]

Methods of Class

1. **mkdir:** This function creates a new directory. We can also provide access to the new directory.

   ```
   Dir.mkdir "dir-name", permission
   ```

2. **Deleting a directory:** The rmdir, delete, and unlink methods are used to remove a directory; the work of all of these methods is the identical.

   ```
   Dir.delete "dir-name"
   Dir.rmdir "dir-name"
   Dir.unlink " Dir-name"
   ```

3. **exist?:** The exist? method may use to determine whether or not a directory exists. It returns a true or false result.

   ```
   Dir.exist?"dir-name"
   ```

4. **pwd:** The pwd (present working directory) technique is used to determine the current working directory.

   ```
   Dir.pwd
   ```

5. **chdir:** The chdir technique is used to modify the current working directory. Using this technique, we may just give the path to the directory that we want to relocate.

   ```
   Dir.chdir "path"
   ```

   The string parameter specifies the absolute or relative path in the chdir procedure.

6. **entries:** To see what is in a directory. It offers a wide range of content.

   ```
   Dir.entries"dir-name" #[".", "..", "file1.txt",
   "another directory"]
   ```

7. **getwd:** This function returns the current working directory path.

   ```
   Dir.getwd
   ```

8. **home:** This function returns the current user's home directory.

```
Dir.home
```

9. **glob:** This approach is used to find a certain file in the current directory. It is based on the pattern-matching notion. It extends a pattern, such as an array of patterns or a string pattern, and returns the matching result. The following notations are used in the glob method:

- *: It applies to all files.
- c*: It matches files that begin with the letter c.
- *c: It matches files that finish in c.
- *c*: It matches all files that contain the letter c, including the beginning and end.
- **: It recursively matches directories.
- ?: It corresponds to any single character.
- [set]: It can match any character in the set.
- {p, q}: It matches either a p or a q literal.
- \: It evades the following metacharacter.

```
Dir.glob("pattern")
```

Instance Methods

The object of the dir class is h_o in this case.

1. **close:** This command is used to terminate the directory stream.

```
h_o.close
```

2. **each:** In each method, the block must be executed once for each entry in the directory, and the filename for each entry should be sent to the block as an argument.

```
each{|filename|block}
```

3. **fileno:** This method is used to give the file number used in dir or to provide the file information in integer value.

```
h_o.fileno
```

4. **path:** The path argument is returned by this procedure.

```
h_o.path
```

5. **pos:** The current position argument is returned by this procedure.

```
h_o.pos=integer
```

6. **read:** This function reads the next directory item and returns it as a string.

```
h_o.read
```

7. **tell:** This function displays the current position in dir.

```
h_o.tell
```

8. **seek:** Use this function to find a specified point in dir. It returns the value as an integer.

```
h_o.seek(integer)
```

9. **Rewind:** This function is used to return dir to its original position.

```
h_o.rewind
```

MATCHDATA CLASS IN RUBY

All pattern matching in Ruby is performed with the help of the special variable $~. All pattern matches will set the $~ to a MatchData that provides match information. The Regexp#match and Regexp.last_match functions return MatchData objects. The MatchData objects included all of the pattern match results, which are generally accessible by the special variables $&, $', $', $1, $2, and so on.[11]

Instance Method

The object of the MatchData Class is called match in this case.

- []: This is referred to as a Match Reference. This MatchData operates like an array and may be accessed using the standard array indexing mechanism. [0] is equivalent to the special variable $& in this match, and it returns the entire matched string. Return the reference value of match[1], match[2], match[3], and so on.

```
match[i]
match[start, length]
match[range]
```

Example:

```
# program to illustrate
# the use of []

# Using the [] operator
a = /(.)(.)(\d+)(\d)/.match("PeeksFORpeeks12.")
a[0]
a[1, 4]
a[1..2]
a[-2, 1]
```

- **begin:** The offset of the start of the nth member of the match array in the string is returned by this method.

```
match.begin(n)
```

Example:

```
# program to illustrate
# the use of begin method

# Using the begin method
a = /(.)(.)(\d+)(\d)/.match("PeeksFORpeeks112.")
a.begin(1)
a.begin(2)
```

- **captures:** This function returns an array containing all of the matched groups.

```
match.captures
```

Example:

```
# program to illustrate
# the use of captures method

# Using the captures method
a = /(.)(.)(\d+)(\d)/.match("PeeksFORpeeks112.")
a.captures
```

- **end:** This function returns the offset into the character in the string that comes directly after the end of the nth entry of the match array.

```
match.end(n)
```

Example:

```
# program to illustrate
# the use of end method

# Using the end method
a = /(.)(.)(\d+)(\d)/.match("PeeksFORpeeks112.")
a.end(0)
a.end(2)
```

- **length:** The length of the match array is returned by this function.

```
match.length
```

Example:

```
# program to illustrate
# the use of length method

# Using the length method
a = /(.)(.)(\d+)(\d)/.match("PeeksFORpeeks112.")
a.length

# using the size method
a.size
```

- **offset:** This function returns a two-element array with the nth match's starting and ending offsets.

```
match.offset(n)
```

Example:

```
# program to illustrate
# the use of offset method

# Using the offset method
a = /(.)(.)(\d+)(\d)/.match("PeeksFORpeeks112.")
a.offset(2)
a.offset(1)
```

- **post_match:** This function returns the portion of the original string that was left over after the current match; the same as the special variable $'.

```
match.post_match
```

Example:

```
# program to illustrate
# the use of post_match method

# Using the post_match method
a = /(.)(.)(\d+)(\d)/.match("PeeksFORpeeks112:
Ruby")
a.post_match
```

- **pre_match:** Returns the portion of the original string preceding the current match; the same as the special variable $'.

```
match.pre_match
```

Example:

```
# program to illustrate
# the use of pre_match method

# Using the pre_match method
a = /(.)(.)(\d+)(\d)/.match("PeeksFORpeeks112:
Ruby")
a.pre_match
```

- **select:** This method returns an array containing all of the items of match where the block is true.

```
match.select{|val|block}
```

- **size:** The size is equivalent to the MatchData#length function.

```
match.size
```

- **string:** Returns a frozen copy of the string provided in the match.

```
match.string
```

Example:

```
# program to illustrate
# the use of string method

# Using the string method
a = /(.)(.)(\d+)(\d)/.match("PeeksFORpeeks112:
Ruby")
a.string
```

- **to_a:** The array of matches is returned by this function.

  ```
  match.to_a
  ```

  Example:

  ```
  # program to illustrate
  # the use of to_a method

  # Using the to_a method
  a = /(.)(.)(\d+)(\d)/.match("PeeksFORpeeks112:
  Ruby")
  a.to_a
  ```

- **to_s:** This function returns the entire matched string.

  ```
  match.to_s
  ```

  Example:

  ```
  # program to illustrate
  # the use of to_s method

  # Using the to_s method
  a = /(.)(.)(\d+)(\d)/.match("PeeksFORpeeks112:
  Ruby")
  a.to_s
  ```

- **values_at:** The index is utilized in this function to retrieve the matching values and return an array of associated matches.

  ```
  match.valu_at([index]*)
  ```

  Example:

  ```
  # program to illustrate
  # the use of values_at method

  # Using the values_at method
  a = /(.)(.)(\d+)(\d)/.match("PeeksFORpeeks112:
  Ruby")
  a.values_at(2, 0)
  ```

- **==:** Equality is the term for this. It is used to determine whether or not both MatchData, that is, match1 and match2, are identical. Return true if they are equal; else, return false.

  ```
  match1==match2
  ```

This chapter covered regular expressions, search and replace, and the many sorts of Ruby classes (Float, integer, Symbol, Struct). Furthermore, we covered the Dir class and its methods, as well as the MatchData class.

NOTES

1. Ruby | Regular expressions: https://www.geeksforgeeks.org/ruby-regular-expressions/, accessed on August 30, 2022.
2. Ruby – regular expressions: https://www.tutorialspoint.com/ruby/ruby_regular_expressions.htm, accessed on August 30, 2022.
3. Ruby search and replace: https://www.geeksforgeeks.org/ruby-search-and-replace/, accessed on August 30, 2022.
4. Ruby | Float class: https://www.geeksforgeeks.org/ruby-float-class/, accessed on August 30, 2022.
5. Useful methods in float class in Ruby: https://www.tutorialspoint.com/useful-methods-in-float-class-in-ruby, accessed on August 30, 2022.
6. Ruby | Integer class: https://www.geeksforgeeks.org/ruby-integer-class/, accessed on August 31, 2022.
7. Useful methods of integer class in Ruby: https://www.tutorialspoint.com/useful-methods-of-integer-class-in-ruby, accessed on August 31, 2022.
8. Ruby | Symbol class: https://www.geeksforgeeks.org/ruby-symbol-class/, accessed on August 31, 2022.
9. Ruby | Struct class: https://www.geeksforgeeks.org/ruby-struct-class/, accessed on August 31, 2022.
10. Dir class and its methods: https://www.geeksforgeeks.org/ruby-dir-class-and-its-methods/, accessed on August 31, 2022.
11. Ruby | MatchData class: https://www.geeksforgeeks.org/ruby-matchdata-class/, accessed on August 31, 2022.

## CHAPTER 8

Module and Collections in Ruby

IN THIS CHAPTER

- ➤ Modules

- ➤ Arrays

- ➤ String Basics

- ➤ Ruby | Hashes Basics

- ➤ Ruby | Blocks

In the previous chapter, we covered regex and classes in Ruby, and in this chapter, we will discuss module and collections in Ruby.

MODULE IN RUBY

A module is made up of methods, constants, and class variables. Modules are created as classes using the module keyword rather than the class keyword.[1]

Important Module Information

- We cannot inherit modules or build subclasses of modules.

- A module cannot use to generate objects.

- Modules are used to create namespaces and mixins.

 DOI: 10.1201/9781003358510-8

- All classes are modules, but not all modules are classes.

- Although the class may utilize namespaces, it cannot use mixins like modules.

- A module's name must begin with a capital letter.

Syntax:

```
module Module-name

    # statements to execute

end
```

Example:

```
# program to illustrate
# module

# Create a module with name Pfp
module Pfp

    C = 20;

    # Prefix with the name of Module
    # module method
    def Pfp.portal
        puts "Welcome to PFP Portal!"
    end

    # Prefix with name of the Module
    # module method
    def Pfp.tutorial
        puts "The Ruby Tutorial"
    end

    # Prefix with name of the Module
    # module method
    def Pfp.topic
        puts "The Topic - Module"
    end

end
```

```
# display the value of
# module constant
puts Pfp::C

# call the methods of the module
Pfp.portal
Pfp.tutorial
Pfp.topic
```

Note:

- When defining a module method, the user must precede the name of the module with the method name. The benefit of constructing module methods is that anyone may call them just by using the module name and the dot operator, as seen in the prior example.

- As illustrated in the above instance, a user can obtain the value of a module constant by using the double colon operator (::).

- If a user defines a method using the def keyword exclusively within a module, for example, def method_name, it is considered an instance method. Because the user cannot create an instance of the module, he cannot access instance methods directly using the dot operator.

- The user must include the module inside a class and then use the class instance to access the instance method provided within the module. The examples below clearly demonstrate this notion.

- The included keyword allows the user to utilize the module within the class. In this situation, the module functions similarly to a namespace.

Example:

```
# program to illustrate how
# to use the module inside a class

# Create a module with name Gfg
module Pfp

    # the module method
    def portal
```

```ruby
        puts "Welcome to PFP Portal!"
    end

    # the module method
    def tutorial
        puts "The Ruby Tutorial!"
    end

    # the module method
    def topic
        puts "The Topic - Module"
    end

end

# Create the class
class PeeksforPeeks

    # Include module in the class
    # by using the 'include' keyword
    include Pfp

    # Method of class
    def add
        x = 40 + 10
        puts x
    end

end

# Create the objects of class
obj_class = PeeksforPeeks.new

# call module methods
# with the help of PeeksforPeeks
# class object
obj_class.portal
obj_class.tutorial
obj_class.topic

# Call class method
obj_class.add
```

USE OF MODULES

Modules are used to organize methods and constants so that they may be reused by the user. Assume we want to develop two methods and then utilize them in numerous apps. So, we will put these functions in a module so that he can simply call it in any program using the need keyword without having to rewrite code.[2]

Example:

```
# program for creating a module

# define the module
module Pfp

    # the module method
    def Pfp.portal()

        puts "The Module Method 1"
    end

    # the module method
    def Pfp.tutorial()

        puts "The Module Method 2"
    end

end
```

Note: Save this code in a file called myeg.rb. We may include this into another code by using the need keyword. This is equivalent to include header files in a C/C++ code.

Using the Command
```
ruby myeg.rb
```

Example:

```
# program to show how to use a
# module using the require keyword

# adding the module
require "./myeg.rb"
```

```
# call the methods of module Pfp
Pfp.portal()
Pfp.tutorial()
```

COMPARABLE MODULE IN RUBY

In Ruby, the class whose objects may be sorted using the Comparable mixin. The class must provide an operation that compares the receiver to another object. Depending on the receiver, it will return −1, 0, or 1. It returns −1 if the receiver is less than another object, and 0 if the receiver is equal to another object.[3] It returns 1 if the receiver is greater than another object. Comparable module employs <=> to implement the standard comparison operators (<, <=, ==, >=, and >) as well as the function between?

Example:

```
# program to illustrate
# the comparable module

class Peeksforpeeks

# include the comparable module
include Comparable
attr :name

    def <=>(other_name)
        name.length <=> other_name.name.length
    end

    def initialize(name)
        @name = name
    end
end

# create objects
a1 = Peeksforpeeks.new("P")
a2 = Peeksforpeeks.new([3, 5])
a3 = Peeksforpeeks.new("peeks")

# using the comparable operator
p a1 < a2
```

```
# using the between? method
p a2.between?(a1, a3)
p a3.between?(a1, a2)
```

Instance Method

- <: It compares two objects depending on the method of the receiver and returns true if it returns −1, else returns false.

    ```
    ob<other_ob
    ```

- <=: It compares two objects depending on the method of the receiver and returns true if it returns −1 or 0, else it returns false.

    ```
    ob<=other_ob
    ```

- ==: It compares two objects depending on the method of the receiver and returns true if it returns 0, else false.

    ```
    obj==other_obj
    ```

- >: It compares two objects depending on the method of the receiver and returns true if it returns 1, else returns false.

    ```
    obj>other_obj
    ```

- >=: compares two objects based on the method of the receiver and returns true if it returns 1 or 0, otherwise returns false.

    ```
    obj>=other_obj
    ```

    Example:

    ```
    # program to illustrate
    # the use of comparisons

    # define class
    class Peeksforpeeks

    # include the comparable module
    include Comparable
    attr :name

        def <=>(other_name)
            name.length <=> other_name.name.length
        end
    ```

```
    def initialize(name)
        @name = name
    end
end

# create objects
a1 = Peeksforpeeks.new("P")
a2 = Peeksforpeeks.new("peeks")

# using the < operator
p a1 < a2

# using the <= operator
p a1 <= a2

# using the == operator
p a1 == a2

# using the >= operator
p a1 >= a2

# using the > operator
p a1 > a2
```

- **between?:** This function returns false if the object <=> min is less than or higher than zero. If not, it returns true.

```
obj.between?(min, max)
```

Example:

```
# program to illustrate
# the use of between? method

# using the between? method
p 7.between?(2, 6)
p 'peeks'.between?('peeks', 'pfp')
```

MATH MODULE IN RUBY

Modules are created in Ruby as a grouping of methods, classes, and constants. The math module includes techniques for fundamental trigonometric and transcendental functions.[4]

Constants in Modules

Name	Description
E	Define the value of the natural logarithm's base e
PI	Determine the value of

Example:

```
# code to illustrate the
# the Math Module constants
puts Math::E

puts Math::PI
```

Methods for Modules

- **acos:** This method computes the arc cosine of a given value *a*. It returns values in the range [0..PI]. This method's return type is float.

```
Math.acos(a)
```

  Example:

```
# code to illustrate
# the acos method
puts Math.acos(0)

# check its range
puts Math.acos(0) == Math::PI/2
```

- **acosh:** This technique computes the inverse hyperbolic cosine of a given value *a*. This function returns a float.

```
Math.acosh(a)
```

- **asin:** This technique computes the arc sine of a given value *a*. It returns values in the range [-PI/2..PI/2]. This function returns a float.

```
Math.asin(a)
```

- **asinh:** This technique computes the inverse hyperbolic sine of a given value *a*. This function returns a float.

```
Math.asinh(a)
```

Example:

```
# code to illustrate
# the asinh method
puts Math.asinh(2)
```

- **atan:** This technique computes the arc of tangent of given value *a*. It produces a result within the range [−PI...PI]. The float is the method's return type.

```
Math.atan(a)
```

- **atanh:** This technique computes the inverse hyperbolic tangent of a given value. This method's return type is float.

```
Math.atanh(a)
```

Example:

```
# code to illustrate
# the atanh method
puts Math.atanh(0.5)
```

- **atan2:** This technique computes the arc of tangent of two values, *a* and *b*. It produces a result within the range [−PI...PI]. This method's return type is float.

```
Math.atan2(a, b)
```

- **cos:** This method computes the cosine of a given number an in radians and returns a value in the range [−1.0...1.0]. This method's return type is float.

```
Math.cos(a)
```

Example:

```
# code to illustrate
# the cos method
puts Math.cos(1)
```

- **cosh:** This technique computes the hyperbolic cosine of a given value an in radians. This method's return type is float.

```
Math.cosh(a)
```

- **erf:** Returns the error function for the given value *a*. This method's return type is float.

```
Math.erf(a)
```

- **erfc:** Returns the complementary error function for the specified value *a*. This method's return type is float.

```
Math.erfc(a)
```

- **exp:** This method returns the value of ea. This method's return type is float.

```
Math.exp(a)
```

Example:

```
# code to illustrate
# the exp method
puts Math.exp(2)
```

- **frexp:** This method returns a two-element array containing the normalized fraction and numeric exponent.

```
Math.frexp(numeric)
```

- **hypot:** This approach yields $\sqrt{a^2 + b^2}$. Alternatively, it yields the hypotenuse of a right-angle triangle with sides *a* and *b*. This method's return type is float.

```
Math.hypot(a, b)
```

Example:

```
# code to illustrate
# the hypot method
puts Math.hypot(5,6)
```

- **Idexp:** This method returns the float * 2 integer value. This method's return type is float.

```
Math.Idexp(float, integer)
```

- **log:** The natural logarithm of numeric is returned by this method. This method's return type is float.

```
Math.log(numeric)
```

- **log10:** This function returns the numeric logarithm in base 10. This method's return type is float.

```
Math.log10(numeric)
```

- **sin:** This technique computes the sine of a numeric value and expresses it in radians. It returns values in the range [−1.0..1.0]. This method's return type is float.

```
Math.sin(numeric)
```

Example:

```
# code to illustrate the
# the sin method
puts Math.sin(0)
```

- **sinh:** This technique computes the hyperbolic sine of a number in radians. This method's return type is float.

```
Math.sinh(numeric)
```

- **sqrt:** If numeric is less than zero, it gives the non-negative square root and issues an ArgError. This method's return type is float.

```
Math.sqrt(numeric)
```

- **tan:** The tangent of an integer in radians is returned by this function. This method's return type is float.

```
Math.tan(numeric)
```

- **tanh:** This technique computes the hyperbolic tangent of a number in radians. This method's return type is float.

```
Math.tanh(numeric)
```

Example:

```
# code to illustrate
# the tanh method
puts Math.tanh(1)
```

INCLUDE VERSUS EXTEND IN RUBY

Include is a module code importer. When we try to use the methods of the import module using the class directly, Ruby will give an error since it is imported as a subclass for the superclass. As a result, the only method to get to it is through the class instance.

Extend is likewise used to import module code, but it does so as class methods.[5] When we try to access methods of the import module with the instance of the class, Ruby will give an error since the module is imported to the superclass exactly like the instance of the extended module. As a result, the only method to get to it is through the class definition.

In basic terms, the distinction between include and extend is that include adds methods solely to a class's instance, whereas extend adds methods to the class but not to its instance.[6]

Example:

```
# program of Include and Extend

# Create a module contains a method
module Peek
def peeks
    puts 'PeeksforPeeks!'
end
end


class Lord

# only can access peek methods
# with the instance of class.
include Peek
end


class Star

# only can access peek methods
# with class definition.
extend Peek
end

# object access
Lord.new.peeks

# class access
Star.peeks

# NoMethodError: undefined method
# 'peeks' for Lord:Class
Lord.peeks
```

If we need to import instance methods and class methods on a class. We can "include" and "expand" it simultaneously.

Example:

```
# program to understand include and extend

# Create a module that contains a method
module Peek
def prints(x)
    puts x
end
end

class PFP

# by using the both include and extend
# we can find them by both instances and
  class name
include Peek
extend Peek
end

# access prints() in Peek
# module by include in the Lord class
PFP.new.prints("Howdy") # object access

# access the prints() in Peek
# module by extend it in the Lord class
PFP.prints("PeeksforPeeks!!") # class access
```

ARRAYS IN RUBY

An array is a group of distinct or related elements stored in adjacent memory regions. The goal is to group together several objects of the same category that may be referred to by a common name.[7]

Numbers, strings, and so on are all basic types in Ruby, but arrays are objects. Arrays are collections of ordered, integer-indexed objects that may store a number, integer, text, hash, symbol, objects, or any other array. In general, an array is built by listing the components separated by commas and contained by square brackets [ ].

Example:

```
["Peeks", 55, 61, "PFP"]
```

Size of array is 4	PFP	55	61	Peeks	Array

	0	1	2	3	Array Positive Index starts from 0

	-4	-3	-2	-1	Array Negative Index starts from -1

Arrays in Ruby.

The array has four distinct types of elements: Peeks (a string), 55 (number), 61 (number), and PFP (string). The array's positive index begins at 0. The negative index always begins with −1, which indicates the entries at the array's end. There can be a two-dimensional array, which stores another array. It is also known as nested arrays. We will just cover one-dimensional arrays in this part.

1D ARRAY CREATION IN RUBY

There are various ways to make an array. However, there are two commonly utilized methods:

- **Using new class method:** The new class method may use to generate arrays using the dot operator. Internally, the:new method with zero, one, or more than one parameters is invoked. Passing parameters to the method involves providing the array's size and items.

  Syntax:

  ```
  Name-of-array= Array.new
  ```

  Example:

  ```
  arr = Array.new
  ```

- The array's name is arr in this case. Array is the preset class name in the Ruby library, while new is the predefined function.

    Note: To determine the size or length of an array, just use the size or length methods. For a given array, both methods will return the same value.

```
arr = Array.new(30)
arr.size
arr.length
```

- The array now has a capacity of 30 elements. The array's size and length are both 30 in this case.

Example:

```
# program to demonstrate the
# create of array using new method and
# to find size and length of array

# create array using new method without
# passing any parameter
arr = Array.new()

# create array using new method passing
# one parameter i.e. the
# size of array
arr2 = Array.new(7)

# create array using new method passing
# two parameters i.e. the
# size of the array & element of array
arr3 = Array.new(4, "PFP")

# display the size of arrays using
# size and length method
puts arr.size
puts arr2.length
puts arr3.size

# display array elements
puts "#{arr3}"
```

- **Using the literal constructor[]:** In Ruby, [] is referred to as the literal constructor, and it may use to create arrays. An array can allocate various or comparable type values between [].[8]

  Example:

  ```
  # program to demonstrate the
  # create of array using literal
  # constructor[] and to find size
  # and length of the array

  # create array of the characters
  arr = Array['h', 'b', 'i', 'd','e', 'f']

  # display array elements
  puts "#{arr}"

  # display array size
  puts "The Size of arr is: #{arr.size}"

  # display array length
  puts "The Length of arr is: #{arr.length}"
  ```

Elements from an Array Are Retrieved or Accessed

There are numerous ways to extract elements from an array in Ruby. Ruby arrays provide several techniques for accessing array elements. However, the most common method is to utilize an array's index.

Example:

```
# program to demonstrate the
# accessing elements of the array

# create string using []
str = ["PFP", "P4P", "Sudo", "Peeks"]

# accessing the array elements
# using index
puts str[1]

# using negative index
puts str[-1]
```

Retrieving Numerous Elements from an Array

Sometimes, a user needs to access multiple components from an array. To access the multiple items, enter the two array indexes into the [].

Example:

```
# program to demonstrate the
# accessing multiple elements
# from array

# create string using []
str = ["PFP", "P4P", "Sudo", "Peeks"]

# accessing the multiple array elements
puts str[2,3]
```

Note: If the user attempts to access an item that does not present in the array, nil will be returned.

Example:

```
# program to demonstrate accessing
# of the array element that doesn't exist

# create array using []
arr = [1, 2, 3, 4]

# accessing index which
# doesn't exist
puts arr[4]
```

The output will include nothing.

STRING BASICS IN RUBY

A string in Ruby is a series of one or more characters. It might be made up of numbers, letters, or symbols. Strings are the objects in this case, and unlike other languages, strings are changeable, which means they may be modified in place rather than producing new strings.[9] The String object stores and manipulates an arbitrary series of bytes, often representing a sequence of characters.

String Creation

String creation is as simple as putting the series of characters in double or single quotes. The user can also store the string in a variable. There is no need to define the variable's data type in Ruby.

Example:

```
# Ruby program to demonstrate
# the creation of strings

# using the single quotes
puts 'String using single quotes in Ruby'

# using the double quotes
puts "String using double quotes in Ruby"

# storing string into the variables
str1 = "PFP"
str2 = 'Peeks'

# display string
puts str1
puts str2
```

Note: The only difference with using single and double quoting is that double quotes may interpolate variables whereas single quotes cannot.

Example:

```
# program to demonstrate the difference
# while using the single and double quotes to
create strings

# storing string into the variables
str1 = "PFP"
str2 = 'Peeks'

# using the single quotes
puts 'The Cannot Interpolate str1: #{str1}'

# using the double quotes
puts "The Interpolating str2: #{str2}"
```

Strings Are Objects

Because Ruby is an object-oriented language, strings in Ruby are objects. An object is essentially a collection of data and procedures that increase the communication feature.

Example:

```
# program to illustrate that string
# are objects in Ruby

#!/usr/bin/ruby

# using the double quotes
str = "PeeksforPeeks"

puts str

# using the new method to create
# string object and assign value to it
str2 = String.new "PeeksforPeeks"

puts str2
```

String Elements Accessible

The string elements can access by using the square brackets []. The user can pass strings, ranges, or indices between square brackets [].

Syntax:

```
name-of-string-variable[arguments]
```

Example:

```
# program to illustrate the
# access of string

#!/usr/bin/ruby

# store string in a variable
str = "PeeksforPeeks Sudo Placements"

# access the specified substring
puts str["Peeks"]
puts str['for']
```

```
# pass index as an argument that returns the
# specified character
puts str[3]

# pass the negative index as an argument which
returns
# the specified character from
# the last of the string
puts str[-3]

# pass Two arguments which are separated by a
# comma that returns characters starting from
# the 1st index and the 2nd index is the number of
characters
puts str[13, 10]

# using the range operators in the pass arguments
puts str[13. . 17]
```

Generating Multiline Strings

In Ruby, a user can simply construct multiline strings; however, in other computer languages, this needs a lot of effort. In Ruby, there are three ways to produce multiline strings:

- Using Double Quotations (""), Simply inserting the string between the quotations is the easiest approach to make multiline strings. The user can insert the newline character between double quotes and so forth.

- Using (%/ /), Simply place the string between the %/ and /to make a multiline string.

- Making use of (<< STRING STRING), simply place the string between the << STRING and STRING to make a multiline string. STRING should capitalize here.

Example:

```
# program to illustrate
# the multiline strings

#!/usr/bin/ruby
```

```
# Using the Double Quotes
puts "A user can create multiline
    strings easily where in the other programming
    languages creation of multiline strings
    requires a lot of the efforts in Ruby"

puts ""

# Using %/ /
puts %/ A user can create multiline
    strings easily where into the other
programming
    languages creation of multiline strings
    requires a lot of the efforts in Ruby/

puts ""

# Using <<STRING STRING
puts <<STRING

A user can create multiline
strings easily where into the other programming
languages creation of multiline strings
requires a lot of efforts in Ruby
STRING
```

String Replication

A user may need to repeat a string several times at times. In order to replicate a string in Ruby, use the (*) operator. The string to be duplicated is preceded by this operator, which is accompanied by the number of times to produce replicas.

Syntax:

```
string-variable-or-string * number-of-times
```

Example:

```
# program to illustrate
# the replication of strings

#!/usr/bin/ruby
```

```
# string to replicate
str = "PeeksForPeeks\n"

# using the * operator
puts str * 7
```

STRING INTERPOLATION IN RUBY

String interpolation is all about merging strings, but not using the + operator. String interpolation works only when the string is formed with double quotations (""). String interpolation makes it simple to parse String literals.[10] String interpolation is the substitution of defined variables or expressions in a given String with respected values. String Interpolation functions in this way: it runs whatever is operable.

Let's look at how to run numbers and strings.

Syntax:

```
#{variable}
```

The syntax above indicates that the contents are executable objects or variables.

Here are some examples to help us understand:

Example:

```
# Program of String Interpolation
m = 1
n = 4
puts "Number #{m} is less than #{n}"
```

Example:

```
# Program of String Interpolation

s = 'Adhik';
n = 17

# takes this as the entire new string
puts "s age = n";

# the interpolation
puts "#{s} age=#{n}";
```

```
# if the number not converted to string throws
error
puts s+" age="+n.to_s;
```

So, the sole advantage is that we don't have to convert integers to strings because Ruby does it for us.

Assume string="weds." If we concatenate strings like ("sona "+string+" sham"), it creates three string objects. Moving from right to left, it first creates "sham" object1, + method sticks the sham with the existing string together and returns weds sham object2, and this is again stuck by + method and forms the final sona weds sham object3. Eventually, the objects(1, 2) generated in this process are terminated since they are no longer useful.

Escape Sequences

Strings can include more than just text. They may also include control characters. The distinction between a single and double quote is that double quotes support escape sequences, whereas single quotes do not.[11]

Example:

```
# program of sting Interpolation
puts 'guardians\nAdhik';

# gets executes and prints the Groot on a newline.
puts "guardians\nAdhik";

# takes care of the control characters.
puts "sona\nweds\tsham";
```

HASHES BASICS IN RUBY

The Hash is a data structure that holds a collection of items known as keys, each with its own value. A hash is just a set of unique keys and their values. Hashes are commonly referred to as associative arrays since they associate values with each key; however, there is a distinction between hashes and arrays.[12] For indexing, arrays always use an integer value, whereas hashes utilize an object. Because they map keys to values, hashes are also called maps.

Hash Literals or Generating Hashes

A hash is formed by using a hash literal, which is a comma-separated list of key/value pairs that are always surrounded by curly braces {}. There are several techniques to generate a hash:

- **Introducing a new class function**

The new class function will generate an empty hash, implying that the hash will have no default value.

Syntax:

```
Hash-variable = Hash.new
```

Example:

```
peeks = Hash.new
```

As a result, empty hash peeks will generate. We may also provide peeks with the default value in two ways:

```
peeks = Hash.new("PFP")
```

or

```
peeks = Hash.new "PFP"
```

PFP is the default value here. When a key or value does not exist in the hash mentioned above, accessing the hash returns the default value "PFP." To give key/value pairs, you must adjust the hash values, as mentioned further below:

- **Using {} braces:** In this hash variable, = and curly braces {} are used. The key/value pairs are constructed between curly braces {}.

Syntax:

```
hash-variable = {"key1" => value1, "key2" => value2}
```

Obtaining Hash Values

To obtain a hash value, always include the appropriate key in square brackets [].

Example:

```
# program to demonstrate the creation
# of the hashes and fetching hash values

#!/usr/bin/ruby

# Create a hash using the new class method
# without default value
geeks = Hash.new

# empty hash will return nothing on the display
puts "#{peeks[4]}"

# create hash using the new class
# method providing a default value
# this could be written as
# peeks = Hash.new "PFP"
geeks_default = Hash.new("PFP")

# it will return PFP for every index of the hash
puts "#{peeks_default[0]}"
puts "#{peeks_default[7]}"

# create hash using {} braces
peeks_hash1 = {"DS" => 1, "Java" => 2}

# fetching the values of hash using []
puts peeks_hash1['DS']
puts peeks_hash1['Java']
```

Modifying Hashes

An existing hash can be updated by adding or removing a key value/pair. We may also alter the value of the key in the hash.

Example:

```
# program to demonstrate modifying of hash

#!/usr/bin/ruby

# create hash using {} braces
peeks_hash1 = {"DS" => 1, "Java" => 2}
```

```
puts "Before Modify"

# fetching the values of hash using []
puts peeks_hash1['DS']
puts peeks_hash1['Java']

puts "\n"

puts "After Modify"

# modify hash values
peeks_hash1["DS"] = 4
peeks_hash1["Java"] = 5

# fetching the values of hash using []
puts peeks_hash1['DS']
puts peeks_hash1['Java']
```

Note: If a user enters two distinct values for the same key in a hash, the prior value is replaced by the current value of the key. In addition, the application will execute correctly but will provide a warning, as demonstrated in the sample below:

```
# program to demonstrate modifying hash

#!/usr/bin/ruby

# create hash using {} braces providing
# two different values to key "DS"
peeks_hash1 = {"DS" => 1, "DS" => 4,"Java" => 2}

puts "Before Modify"

# fetching the values of hash using []
puts peeks_hash1['DS']
puts peeks_hash1['Java']

puts "\n"

puts "After Modify"
```

```
# modify hash values
peeks_hash1["DS"] = 4
peeks_hash1["Java"] = 5

# fetching the values of hash using []
puts peeks_hash1['DS']
puts peeks_hash1['Java']
```

HASH CLASS IN RUBY

Hash is a set of unique keys and their values in Ruby. Hash is similar to an Array, except that it is indexed using arbitrary keys of any object type. The order in which various iterators return keys and their values in Hash is arbitrary and will typically not be in the insertion order.[13] Hashes' default value is nil. When a user attempts to access keys that do not exist in the hash, nil is returned.

Class Method

1. []: This function generates a new hash containing specified items. It is the same as creating a hash with the literal {Key=>value….}. The pair contains both keys and values, resulting in an even number of parameters.

```
Hash[(key=>value)*]
```

Example:

```
# program to illustrate
# the use of []
# Using the []
p Hash["x", 20, "y", 12]
p Hash["x" => 20, "y" => 12]
```

2. new: This method yields a null hash. If a hash is later accessed with a key that does not match the hash entry, the value returned by this method is determined by the style of new used to construct the hash. The access returns nil in the first form. If obj is provided, this object is utilized for all default values. If a block is supplied, the hash key and objects will call it and return the default value. The block determines the values that are saved in the hash (if necessary).

```
Hash.new
Hash.new(obj)
Hash.new{|hash, key|block}
```

Example:

```
# program to illustrate
# the use of new method

# Using the new method
a = Hash.new("peeksforpeeks")
p a["x"] = 30
p a["y"] = 39
p a["x"]
p a["y"]
p a["z"]
```

3. try_convert: This method converts obj to hash and returns the hash or nil. When the obj does not convert to a hash, it returns nil.

```
Hash.try_convert(obj)
```

Example:

```
# program to illustrate
# the use of try_convert method

# Using the try_convert method
p Hash.try_convert({3=>7})
p Hash.try_convert("3=>7")
```

Instance Method

The hsh variable is an instance of the Hash Class in the methods specified below.

1. ==: It is referred to as equality. It is used to determine whether two hashes are equal. If they are equal, which implies they have the same number of keys and the values associated with these keys are equal, it will return true; otherwise, it will return false.

```
hsh1 == hsh2
```

Example:

```
# program to illustrate
# the use of Equality
```

```
m1 = {"x" => 4, "y" => 107}
m2 = {"x" => 67, "f" => 75, "z" => 20}
m3 = {"f" => 78, "x" => 64, "z" => 20}

# Using the equality
p m1 == m2
p m2 == m3
```

2. []: This is referred to as Element Reference. It returns the value contained in the key. The default value is returned if no value is detected.

```
hsh[key]
```

Example:

```
# program to illustrate
# the use of []

m = {"x" => 42, "y" => 61}

# Using []
p m["x"]
p m["z"]
```

3. []=: This is referred to as Element Assignment. It connects the value provided by value to the key provided by key.

```
hsh[key]=value
```

Example:

```
# program to illustrate
# the use of []=

m = {"x" => 42, "y" => 61}

# Using []=
m["x"]= 32
m["z"]= 81
p a
```

4. clear: This function clears the hsh of all keys and values.

```
hsh.clear
```

Example:

```
# program to illustrate
# the use of clear method

m = {"x" => 42, "y" => 61}

# Using clear method
p m.clear
```

5. default: The default value is returned by this function. If the key does not exist in hsh, the value returned by hsh[key].

```
hsh.default(nil=key)
```

Example:

```
# program to illustrate
# the use of default method

m = Hash.new("peeksforpeeks")

# Using the default method
p m.default
p m.default(2)
```

6. default=: This function establishes a default value (the value which is returned for a key and not exists in a hash).

```
hsh.default=obj
```

7. default_proc: If Hash.new was performed with the block, this function will be invoked. If block is returned, else nil is returned.

```
hsh.default_proc
```

Example:

```
# program to illustrate
# the use of default_proc method
```

```ruby
c = Hash.new {|c, v| c[v] = v*v*v}

# Using default_proc method
d = c.default_proc
e = []
p d.call(e, 2)
p e
```

8. delete: By returning the matching value, this function deletes the element from the hash whose key is key. If the key cannot find, this function returns nil. If the optional block is provided and the key is not found, the block will pass and the result of the block will return.

```ruby
hsh.delete(key)
hsh.delete(key) {|key|block}
```

Example:

```ruby
# program to illustrate
# the use of delete method

m = {"x" => 32, "y" => 61}

# Using the delete method
p m.delete("x")
p m.delete("z")
```

9. delete_if: When the block is true, this function deletes the keys and their values from the hsh.

```ruby
hsh.delete_if{|key, value|block}
```

Example:

```ruby
# program to illustrate
# the use of delete_if method

m = {"x" => 32, "y" => 61}

# Using the delete_if method
p m.delete_if {|key, value| key >= "y"}
```

10. each: This function calls block once for each key in hsh, passing key and value as parameters.

```
hsh.each{|key, value|block}
```

Example:

```
# program to illustrate
# the use of each method

m = {"x" => 32, "y" => 61}

# Using the each method
m.each {|key, value| puts "value of #{key} is
#{value}" }
```

11. each_key: This method runs block once for each key in hsh and takes the key as an argument.

```
hsh.each_key{|key|block}
```

Example:

```
# program to illustrate
# the use of each_key method

m = { "x" => 32, "y" => 61 }

# Using each_key method
m.each_key {|key| puts key }
```

12. each_pair: This function is identical to Hash#each.

```
hsh.each_pair{|key, value|block}
```

13. each_value: This method runs block once for every key in hsh and passes value as an argument.

```
hsh.each_key{|value|block}
```

Example:

```
# program to illustrate
# the use of each_value method
```

```
# Using the each_value method
m = { "g" => 22, "h" => 21, "x"=>1234, "y"=>1263,
"z"=>526 }
m.each_value{|value| puts value }
```

14. empty?: This method returns true if hsh contains no key-value pairs. Return false otherwise.

```
hsh.empty?
```

15. fetch: Using the provided key, this function returns a value from the hsh. If the key cannot discover, the following requirements must meet:

- If there is no argument, it will throw an exception.

- If the default is specified, the default will return.

- If an option block is available, it will execute the block and return the result.

There is no default value in the fetch method. When the hash is generated, it will only look for keys that are present in the hash.

```
hsh.fetch(key[, default])
hsh.fetch(key){|key|block}
```

16. has_key?: If provided key is present in the hsh, this method returns true; otherwise, it returns false.

```
hsh.has_key?
```

Example:

```
# program to illustrate
# the use of has_key? method

m = {"g" => 24, "h" => 26, "x"=>2452, "y"=>3651,
"z"=>615}

# Using the has_key? method
p m.has_key?("x")
p m.has_key?("p")
```

17. has_value?: If the specified value exists for a key in the hsh, this method returns true; otherwise, it returns false.

```
hsh.has_value?
```

Example:

```
# program to illustrate
# the use of has_value? method

m = { "g" => 24, "h" => 27, "x"=>4431, "y"=>2453,
"z"=>613 }

# Using the has_value? method
p m.has_value?(24)
p m.has_value?(254)
```

18. include?: This technique is equivalent to the Hash#has_key? function.

```
hsh.include?
```

19. index: This method returns the key containing the specified value. If many keys contain the provided value, it will return just one key from all keys and nil if not found. This is an outdated approach. As a result, we must use Hash#key instead.

```
hsh.index(value)
```

20. invert: This function returns a new hash with the values of hsh as keys and the keys as values. If duplicate values are identified, it will include just one value that is the key among all the values.

```
hsh.invert
```

Example:

```
# program to illustrate
# the use of invert method

m = { "g" => 21, "h" => 24, "x"=>2442, "y"=>4413,
"z"=>274 }
```

```
# Using the invert method
p m.invert
```

21. This is a function comparable to Hash#has key?

```
hsh.key?(key)
```

22. keys: This function returns an array of the hash's keys.

```
hsh.keys
```

23. length: This function returns the number of key-value pairs in the hsh.

```
hsh.length
```

Example:

```
# program to illustrate
# the use of length method

m = {"g" => 24, "h" => 26}

# Using length method
p m.length
```

24. member?: It is a method comparable to Hash#has key?

```
hsh.member?(key)
```

25. merge: This function returns a new hash including the content of other hsh. If a block is supplied, then the hashes and the value stored in the new hash are called for each duplicate key and its value.

```
hsh.merge(other_hsh)
hsh.merge(other_hsh){|key, old_value, new_value|block}
```

Example:

```
# program to illustrate
# the use of merge method
```

```
m1 = { "g" => 21, "h" => 22 }
m2 = { "h" => 2153, "i" => 3350 }

# Using merge method
p m1.merge(m2)
```

26. merge!: This method combines the contents of one hsh with the contents of another hsh, overwriting entries with redundant keys with those from other_hsh.

```
hsh.merge!(other_hsh)
hsh.merge!(other_hsh){|key, old_value,
new_value|block}
```

Example:

```
# program to illustrate
# the use of merge! method

m1 = {"g" => 22, "h" => 26}
m2 = {"h" => 2353, "i" => 5120}

# Using the merge! method
p m1.merge!(m2)

m1 = {"g" => 22, "h" => 26 }

# Using merge! method
p m1.merge!(m2) {|x, y, z| y}
p m1
```

27. rehash: Recreate the hash using the current hash value from each key. If the value of the keys hash changes, the hsh will be re-indexed.

```
hsh.rehash
```

Example:

```
# program to illustrate
# the use of rehash method

x = [ "x", "g" ]
```

```
y = [ "y", "f" ]
m = { x => 32315, y => 5726 }
p m[x]
p x[0] = "h"
p m[x]

# Using the rehash method
p m.rehash
p m[x]
```

28. reject: This function is identical to Hash#delete_if, except it returns a copy of hsh.

```
hsh.reject{|key, value|block}
```

29. reject!: Similar to Hash#delete_if, but returns nil if no changes are made.

```
hsh.reject!{|key, value|block}
```

30. replace: This method replaces the content of hsh with the content of other_hsh.

```
hsh.replace(other_hsh)
```

Example:

```
# program to illustrate
# the use of replace method

m = { "x" => 31, "y" => 50, "z"=>44 }

# Using the replace method
p m.replace({ "y" => 77, "x" => 786 })
```

31. select: This function returns a new array containing a key and value pair for each true condition in the block.

```
hsh.select{|key, value| block}
```

Example:

```
# program to illustrate
# the use of select method
```

```
m = { "x" => 32, "y" => 63, "z"=>31 }

# Using the select method
p m.select {|g, f| g > "x"}
```

32. shift: Removes the key and value pair from the hsh and returns it as a two-item array. If there are no pairs in the hsh, return nil.

```
hsh.shift
```

Example:

```
# program to illustrate
# the use of shift method

m = { "x" => 32, "y" => 62, "z"=>31 }

# Using shift method
p m.shift
p m
```

33. size: This function works in the same way as Hash#length.

```
hsh.size
```

34. sort: This function uses Array#sort to transform the hsh to a nested array of arrays containing keys and values.

```
hsh.sort
hsh.sort{|a, b|block}
```

Example:

```
# program to illustrate
# the use of sort method

m = { "x" => 32, "y" => 61, "z"=>44 }

# Using the sort method
p m.sort
p m.sort {|x, y| x[1]<=>y[1]}
```

35. store: This method works similarly to Hash#[]=.

```
hsh.store(key, value)
```

36. to_a: This method converts the hsh to a nested array of arrays with keys and values.

```
hsh.to_a
```

```
# program to illustrate
# use of the to_a method

a = { "x" => 34, "y" => 60, "z"=>33 }

# Using the to_a method
p a.to_a
```

37. to_s: This function returns a string representation of hsh. In other words, it turns the hash array, which consists of a key and value pair, into a string.

```
hsh.to_s
```

38. update: This technique is comparable to Hash#merge!.

```
hsh.update(other_hsh)
hsh.update(other_hsh){|key, old_value,
new_value|block}
```

39. value?: This function is equivalent to Hash#has value?

```
hsh.value?(value)
```

40. values: This function produces an array containing the values found in hsh.

```
hsh.values
```

41. values_at: This method produces an array containing the values of the given keys as well as default values for keys that cannot find.

```
hsh.values_at([keys])
```

Example:

```
# program to illustrate
# the use of values_at method

m = {"x" => 31, "y" => 63, "z"=>44}

# Using the values_at method
p m.values_at("x", "y")

# Using the default method
m.default = "peeks"

# Using values_at method
p m.values_at("x", "y", "z", "g")
```

BLOCKS IN RUBY

A block is the same as a method, except it is not associated with an object. In other computer languages, blocks are known as closures.[14] There are a few 3Z critical factors to remember regarding Ruby blocks:

- Block is capable of accepting arguments and returning a value.

- Block does not have a unique name.

- A block is made up of code pieces.

- A block is always called by a function or provided to a method call.

- The yield statement invokes a block within a method with a value.

- Blocks, like methods, can be invoked from within the method to which they are provided.

A block code can apply in two ways:

- **Syntax within the do..end statement:**

```
block_name do

    #statement_1
    #statement_2
    .

    .
end
```

Example:

```
# program to demonstrate the block
# defined inside the do..end statements

# here 'each' is method name
# or block name
# n is variable
["Peeks", "PFP", 55].each do |n|
puts n
end
```

- **Syntax of Inline between the curly braces {}:**

```
block_name { #statements-to-be-executed }
```

Example:

```
# program to demonstrate the block
# Inline between curly braces {}

# here 'each' is method name
# n is variable
["Peeks", "PFP", 55].each {|i| puts i}
```

Block Arguments

Arguments can provide to a block by encapsulating them between pipes or vertical bars (| |).

Example:

```
# program to demonstrate
# the arguments passing to block

# india_states is an array and
# it is argument which is to
# pass to block here
india_states = ["Assam", "Bihar", "Andhra
Pradesh", "Chhattisgarh",
                "Goa", "Haryana", "Arunachal
Pradesh", "Manipur",
                "Karnataka", "Gujarat", "Punjab",
"Uttar Pradesh",
                "Uttarakhand"]
```

```
# passing the argument to block
india_states.each do |india_states|
puts india_states
end
```

Explanation: In the preceding example, india_states is the parameter supplied to the block. It's comparable to the def_method name (india_states) here. The main distinction is that function has a name but not a block, and parameters to the method are passed between brackets (), but arguments to block are provided between pipes ||.

How Block Values Are Returned

Block returns the value returned by the method that it is called.

Example:

```
# program to demonstrate how block returns values

# two methods called i.e 'select' and 'even?'
# even? method is called inside the block
puts [1, 2, 3, 4, 5].select { |num| num.even? }
```

Explanation: In the preceding example, there are two methods: select, even?, and a block. The choose method will first call the block for each number in the array. It will first send the 11 to block, and then within the block, there is another method named even? that will accept it as num variable and return false for 11. This false value is sent to the select function, which discards it and then passes 12 to the block. Likewise, inside the block, the odd? method is called, which returns true for the value 12 and this true value is passed to the choose method. This value will now be saved by the choose method. Likewise, for the remaining values in the array, the select method will store the values in the array before returning to the puts function, which publishes the returned array items on the screen.

The Yield Statement

The yield statement uses the yield keyword with a value to call a block within the function.[15]

Example:

```
# program to demonstrate the yield statement

# the method
def shivi

# statement of the method to execute
puts "Inside Method!"

    # using the yield statement
    yield

# statement of the method to execute
puts "Again Inside Method!"

# using the yield statement
yield

end

# block
shivi{puts "Inside Block!"}
```

Explanation: The name of the method in the preceding program is shivi. First, method statements that display Inside Method are called. However, as soon as the yield statements run, control passes to block, which executes its instructions. When the block is executed, control is returned to the method, and the method continues to execute from where the yield statement was called.

Note: It should note that parameters can provide to the yield statement.

Example:

```
# program to demonstrate yield statement

# method
def shivi

# statement of the method to execute
puts "Inside Method!"
```

```
    # using the yield statement
    # p1 is parameter
    yield "p1"

# statement of the method to execute
puts "Again Inside Method!"

# using the yield statement
# p2 is parameter
yield "p2"

end

# block
shivi{ |para| puts "Inside Block #{para}"}
```

BEGIN and END Blocks

In a Ruby code, the BEGIN and END blocks are used to indicate the block of code that will be executed when the file is loaded. The END block will be performed once the program has completed executing. A code may have many BEGIN and END blocks. BEGIN blocks always execute in the same order as END blocks, whereas END blocks operate in the opposite order.

Example:

```
# program to demonstrate BEGIN and END block

#!/usr/bin/ruby

# BEGIN block
BEGIN {

# BEGIN block code
puts "This is the BEGIN block Code"
}

# END block
END {

# END block code
puts "This is the END block code"
}
```

```
# The Code will execute before the END block
puts "Before END block"
```

Note: It should note that we can utilize the same variable both within and outside of a block.

Example:

```
# program to demonstrate the use of
# the same variable outside and inside block

#!/usr/bin/ruby

# variable 'x' outside block
x = "Outside the block"

# here x is inside block
4.times do |x|
puts "Value Inside block: #{x}"
end

puts "Value Outside block: #{x}"
```

Modules, arrays, string basics, hashes basics, and blocks were all covered in this chapter.

NOTES

1. Ruby | Module: https://www.geeksforgeeks.org/ruby-module/, accessed on August 31, 2022.
2. Ruby modules: https://www.javatpoint.com/ruby-modules, accessed on August 31, 2022.
3. Ruby | Comparable module: https://www.geeksforgeeks.org/ruby-comparable-module/, accessed on August 31, 2022.
4. Ruby | Math module: https://www.geeksforgeeks.org/ruby-math-module/, accessed on August 31, 2022.
5. Include vs. extend in Ruby: https://www.geeksforgeeks.org/include-v-s-extend-in-ruby/, accessed on September 01, 2022.
6. Difference between "include" and "extend" in Ruby: https://www.tutorialspoint.com/difference-between-include-and-extend-in-ruby, accessed on September 01, 2022.
7. Ruby | Arrays: https://www.geeksforgeeks.org/ruby-arrays/, accessed on September 01, 2022.

8. Ruby arrays: https://www.javatpoint.com/ruby-arrays, accessed on September 01, 2022.

9. Ruby | String basics: https://www.geeksforgeeks.org/ruby-string-basics/, accessed on September 01, 2022.

10. Ruby | String interpolation: https://www.geeksforgeeks.org/ruby-string-interpolation/, accessed on September 01, 2022.

11. String interpolation: http://ruby-for-beginners.rubymonstas.org/bonus/string_interpolation.html, accessed on September 01, 2022.

12. Ruby | Hashes basics: https://www.geeksforgeeks.org/ruby-hashes-basics/, accessed on September 01, 2022.

13. Ruby | Hash class: https://www.geeksforgeeks.org/ruby-hash-class/, accessed on September 01, 2022.

14. Ruby | Blocks: https://www.geeksforgeeks.org/ruby-blocks/, accessed on September 01, 2022.

15. Ruby – blocks: https://www.tutorialspoint.com/ruby/ruby_blocks.htm, accessed on September 01, 2022.

## CHAPTER 9

Threading in Ruby

IN THIS CHAPTER

➢ Introduction to Multithreading

➢ Thread Class-Public Class Methods

➢ Thread Life Cycle and Its States

In the previous chapter, we covered module and collections in Ruby, and in this chapter, we will discuss threading in Ruby.

INTRODUCTION TO MULTITHREADING

The most beneficial aspect of Ruby is multithreading, which allows the concurrent development of two or more code components to maximize CPU efficiency. Thread refers to each component of a program. Threads, in other terms, are lightweight processes inside processes. A typical program has one thread that runs each command or instruction in turn. While the threads run concurrently on the multicore CPU, a multithreaded code contains several threads, and the statements or instructions inside each thread execute sequentially. Multithreading utilizes less memory than a single thread since it completes more jobs.[1]

Green Threads were employed before Ruby 1.9 to switch threads inside the interpreter. But starting with Ruby 1.9, the operating system is in charge of threading. Ruby programs can never allow two threads to run totally concurrently. The Thread class in Ruby is used to create multithreaded applications, and the block method Thread.new is used to create a new thread.

DOI: 10.1201/9781003358510-9

THREAD CREATION IN RUBY

It is straightforward to start a new thread with Ruby. We can create a thread in a program using one of three blocks (Thread.new, Thread.start, or Thread.fork). The thread is frequently created by using Thread.new. The first thread will return from one of these Thread formation blocks after the thread has been created, continuing processing with the subsequent statement.[2]

Syntax:

```
# The Original thread is running

# create thread
Thread.new
{
    # new thread runs here
}

# Outside block
# The Original thread is running
```

Example:

```
# program to illustrate
# the creation of threads

#!/usr/bin/ruby

# the first method
def Peeks1
a = 0
while a <= 3

    puts "Peeks1: #{a}"

    # to pause the execution of current
    # thread for a specified time
    sleep(1)

    # increment the value of a
    a = a + 1
```

```ruby
end

end

# the Second method
def Peeks2
b = 0

while b <= 3

    puts "Peeks2: #{b}"

    # to pause the execution of current
    # thread for specified time
    sleep(0.5)

    # increment the value of a
    b = b + 1
end

end

# create thread for first method
x = Thread.new{Peeks1()}

# create thread for second method
y= Thread.new{Peeks2()}

# using the Thread.join method to
# wait for the first
# thread to finish
x.join

# using the Thread.join method to
# wait for the second
# thread to finish
y.join

puts "The Process End"
```

Note: Because the operating system allocates resources to threads, the output may change.

TERMINATING THREADS

When a Ruby code is ended, all threads associated with that program are simultaneously terminated. The threads can destroy by using class ::kill.

Syntax:

```
Thread.kill(thread)
```

Thread Variables and Their Scope

Threads have access to local, global, and instance variables specified in the scope of the block since the blocks define them. Variables in the thread block are the thread's local variables and are not accessible by any other thread block. The Thread class enables the creation and access of thread-local variables by name. Thread synchronization is required whenever two or more threads wish to read and write the same variable at the same time.

Example:

```ruby
# program to illustrate
# the Thread variables

#!/usr/bin/ruby

# the Global variable
$str = "PeeksforPeeks"

# the first method
def Peeks1

# only access by Peeks1 Thread
a = 0

while a <= 3

    puts "Peeks1: #{a}"

    # to pause the execution of current
    # thread for a specified time
    sleep(1)

    # incrementing value of a
    a = a + 1

end
```

```ruby
# accessing str
puts "The Global variable: #$str"

end

# the Second method
def Peeks2

# only access by Peeks2 Thread
b = 0

while b <= 3

    puts "Peeks2: #{b}"

    # to pause the execution of current
    # thread for specified time
    sleep(0.5)

    # incrementing value of a
    b = b + 1
end

# accessing str
puts "The Global variable: #$str"

end

# create thread for first method
x = Thread.new{Geeks1()}

# create thread for second method
y= Thread.new{Geeks2()}

# using the Thread.join method to
# wait for first thread
# to finish
x.join

# using the Thread.join method to
# wait for second thread
# to finish
y.join

puts "The Process End"
```

THREAD CLASS-PUBLIC CLASS METHODS IN RUBY

Threads are used in Ruby to implement concurrent coding modules. Threads are used to construct threads in programs that require numerous threads. The Thread class offers a variety of methods that accomplish various functions.[3]

Methods of Public Class

1. abort_on_exception: The state of the global "abort on exception" condition is returned by this method. This method's default value is false. If the value of this method is set to true, all threads in which an exception is thrown are aborted.

```
Thread.abort_on_exception -> true or false
```

2. abort_on_exception=: The new state is returned by this procedure. When the value of this function is set to true, the threads in which the exception occurs are aborted. This method's return type is Boolean.

```
Thread.abort_on_exception= bool -> true or false

# program to illustrate the
# abort_on_exception Method

Thread.abort_on_exception = true

x = Thread.new do

puts "Welcome to the new thread"
raise "The Exception is raised in thread"
end

sleep(0.5)
puts "Not Found"
```

3. critical: The global "thread critical" condition is returned by this procedure.

```
Thread.critical -> true or false
```

4. critical=: This method is used to set and return the global "thread critical" status. When the value of this method is set to true, it prevents the scheduling of any current thread but does not prevent the creation and execution of a new thread. Some thread activities, such as terminating or pausing a thread, sleeping in the current thread, or throwing an exception, may result in a thread being scheduled in a crucial section. This strategy mostly assists those who are creating threading libraries. This method's return type is Boolean.

```
Thread.critical= bool -> true or false
```

5. current: This function returns the thread's current operation.

```
Thread.current -> thread
```

6. exit: This technique is used to terminate the presently executing threads and schedule the execution of another thread. If this thread is marked to be destroyed, it returns the thread; otherwise, if this is the main or final thread, it quits the process.

```
Thread.exit
```

7. fork: This approach is comparable to the start method.

```
Thread.fork{block} -> thread
```

8. kill: This procedure is used to terminate the thread.

```
Thread.kill(thread)
```

Example:

```
# program to illustrate
# the kill Method

counter = 0

# create new thread
x = Thread.new { loop { counter += 1 } }

# using the sleep method
sleep(0.5)

# exits thread using kill method
```

```
Thread.kill(x)

# give it time to die!
sleep(0.6)

# return false
x.alive?
```

9. list: This function returns an array of thread objects representing all threads that are either running or stopped.

```
Thread.list -> array
```

Example:

```
# program to illustrate
# the list Method

# the first thread
Thread.new { sleep(120) }

# the second thread
Thread.new { 12000.times {|z| z*z } }

# the third thread
Thread.new { Thread.stop }

# using the list method
Thread.list.each {|thr| p thr }
```

10. main: This function returns the process's main thread. The application will always return a unique id for each run.

```
Thread.main -> thread

# program to print the id
# of the main thread

# using main method
puts Thread.main
```

11. new: This method creates and runs a new thread to carry out the instruction in the block. The block contains any arguments supplied to this procedure.

```
Thread.new([arguments]*){|arguments|block} -> thread
```

12. pass: This function attempts to pass execution to another thread, but the operating system determines how the execution is switched.

```
Thread.pass
```

13. start: This method is comparable to the new approach. When the Thread class is subclassed, invoking start from subclass does not call the subclass's initialize function.

```
Thread.start([arguments]*){|arguments|block} -> thread
```

14. stop: This function is used to put the current running thread to sleep and schedule the execution of another thread, as well as to reset the critical condition to false.

```
Thread.stop
```

Example:

```
# program to illustrate
# the stop Method

x = Thread.new { print "peeks"; Thread.stop; print
"peeksforpeeks" }

# using the pass method
Thread.pass

print "peeksforpeeks"

x.run
x.join
```

THREAD LIFE CYCLE AND ITS STATES IN RUBY

The Thread life cycle describes the thread from its inception to its demise. Thread.new, Thread.start, and Thread.fork can use to create a new thread. After creation, there is no need to create a new thread. When the CPU's resources are available, a thread begins to execute automatically. Thread. new a citation returns a Thread object as its value. The Thread Class contains several methods for querying and manipulating the thread.[4]

A thread enters the block of code associated to the call to Thread.new and then exits. The outcome of the final expression inside the thread block is the thread's value, which is acquired by using the Thread object's value method. The value method returns value only if the thread has completed its execution; otherwise, it does not deliver value to the thread that has completed its execution. If an exception is thrown in the thread, the running thread is terminated. This condition only applies to threads that are not the main thread and only to threads that end with an exception.

Thread States

In Ruby, threads can be assigned one of five states that indicate the thread's status. The alive? and status methods can use to determine a thread's state.[5]

- **Runnable:** A thread that is now operating or is ready to consume CPU resources when they become available.

- **Sleeping:** A thread that is now sleeping, waiting for IO, or has halted itself.

- **Aborting:** Aborting is a transitional condition. An aborting thread that has been killed but has not yet been terminated.

- **Terminated with exception:** A thread that contains an exception, or a thread that is terminated owing to the occurrence of an exception.

- **Thread that terminated normally:** A thread that did not include an exception and completed its task.

Example:

```
# program to illustrate
# the check status of thread

counter = 0
```

```
# create new thread
m = Thread.new { loop { counter += 1 } }

# check the thread alive or not
puts m.alive?
```

Main Thread

The main thread is a subset of multithreading in Ruby. It is the topmost thread in a code, and all subthreads run under it; in other words, it is the parent thread, and all other threads in the same program are the child threads of the main thread. The main method is used to generate the main thread. When the main thread's job is finished, the Ruby interpreter stops operating, indicating that both the main thread and the child thread have completed their tasks. Thread.main returns the Thread object, which represents the main thread. If an exception is triggered on the main thread and it is not handled anywhere, the Ruby interpreter will either display a message or leave. If an exception is raised on a thread other than the main thread, the Ruby interpreter will terminate the thread containing the exception.

Example:

```
# program to illustrate
# the main thread

# Create the main thread
puts Thread.main
puts ""

# create the new thread
a1 = Thread.new {sleep 230}
list_thread= Thread.list
list_thread.each {|t| p t }
puts "The Current thread = " + Thread.current.to_s

# create the new thread
a2 = Thread.new {sleep 220}
list_thread= Thread.list
list_thread.each {|t| p t }
puts "The Current thread=" + Thread.current.to_s

# kill the thread a1
Thread.kill(a1)
```

```
# pass execution to thread a2
Thread.pass

# kill the thread a2
Thread.kill(a2)

list_thread= Thread.list
list_thread.each {|t| p t }

# exit the main thread
Thread.exit
```

Explanation: This code demonstrates how the main thread runs. First, we construct the main thread, and then within that main thread, we have two subthreads, a1 and a2. When thread a1 has completed its execution, terminate it and send control to thread a2. After that, terminate a2 thread and show a list of all threads in the main thread, along with their status. When all of the threads in the main thread have died, the main thread exists.

Alternate Thread States: Pausing, Waking, and Killing

Threads, as we know, are generated in a runnable state and are ready to run. A thread pauses by entering a sleeping state, invoking the Thread.stop function, or calling Kernel.sleep. A thread cannot force to halt by another thread. If a thread calls Kernel.sleep without an argument, it pauses the thread indefinitely or until it is woken up; if a thread calls Kernel.sleep with an argument, it momentarily puts the thread into a sleeping state. When the timer expires, the thread that is in a temporary sleeping state wakes up and returns to the runnable state.

A thread can pause by invoking Thread.stop or kernel. Sleep can resume by invoking instance methods, i.e. wake up and run. These techniques change a thread's status from sleeping to runnable. A thread scheduler is also called using the run method. The freshly awakened thread may receive CPU resources as a result of the thread scheduler being called. The wakeup function wakes up a single thread without using the thread scheduler.

By executing instance method kill, a thread can forcefully end another thread. The kill technique is comparable to the terminate-and-exit approach. These techniques set the killed method to terminate normally. Killing a thread is risky unless you have a method of confirming that the thread is not in the middle of a file-sharing session. Killing a thread using the! technique is more hazardous since it may leave sockets, files, and other resources open.

We covered introduction to multithreading, thread class-public class methods, and thread life cycle and its states in this chapter.

NOTES

1. Ruby | Introduction to multithreading: https://www.geeksforgeeks.org/ruby-introduction-to-multi-threading/, accessed on September 1, 2022.
2. Ruby thread: https://www.javatpoint.com/ruby-multithreading, accessed on September 1, 2022.
3. Ruby | Thread class-public class methods: https://www.geeksforgeeks.org/ruby-thread-class/, accessed on September 1, 2022.
4. Ruby | Thread life cycle and its states: https://www.geeksforgeeks.org/ruby-thread-life-cycle-its-states/, accessed on September 1, 2022.
5. Thread life cycle and its states in Ruby: https://www.tutorialspoint.com/thread-life-cycle-and-its-states-in-ruby, accessed on September 1, 2022.

Appraisal

Open source, Ruby is a dynamic, object-oriented, and reflective programming language. Programming languages like Perl and Smalltalk are thought to be analogous to Ruby. It runs on every platform, including Windows, Mac OS, and every UNIX variant.

It is a fully object-oriented programming language. Everything is an object in Ruby. Each code has a unique collection of traits and operations. While methods are referred to as actions, variables are referred to as properties.

It is believed that Ruby complies with the POLA principle (principle of least astonishment). It means that the language is designed to avoid confusing seasoned users.

CONCEPT OF RUBY

Perl is considered a toy language even though it is a scripting language. Programming in Python is not entirely object-oriented. A Ruby developer named Yukihiro "Martz" Matsumoto wanted an object-oriented programming language that could also be used for scripting. He searched for this language but was unable to find it. He, therefore, produced one.

THE NAME "RUBY"

Matsumoto and Keiju Ishitsuka's talk inspired the moniker "Ruby." The names "Coral" and "Ruby" were selected. The latter was chosen by Matsumoto since it was a coworker's birthstone.

EARLY YEARS OF RUBY

On December 21, 1995, the first public release of Ruby 0.95 was announced in a Japanese newspaper. The following two days saw the release of three separate versions.

For the Japanese market, Ruby has been modified. The first English-language Ruby mailing list, known as Ruby-Talk, was created to aid in its expansion.

 DOI: 10.1201/9781003358510-10

The first Ruby book, "Programming Ruby," was released in 2001. Following its release, the number of Ruby programmers worldwide rose.

They published their first Ruby framework, "Ruby on Rails," in 2005. The framework release was hugely successful, and the Ruby community grew tremendously.

In May 2008, Ruby 1.8.7 was released. Ruby was at its pinnacle at this period, so much so that even Mac OS X began arriving with built-in Ruby.

RUBY IN PRESENT

Ruby version 2.4.0 was published on Christmas in 2016. It includes various innovative features like hash table improvements, instance variable access, Array#max, and Array#min.

FUTURE OF RUBY

Ruby is an excellent object-oriented high-level programming language. Based on its history, we may conclude that it has a promising future if its members continue to develop it beyond the realm of thought.

CHARACTERISTICS OF RUBY

The Ruby programming language offers several features. Among them are:

- Ruby is an open-source programming language freely available on the Internet, although it is subject to a license.

- Ruby is an interpreted general-purpose programming language.

- Ruby is an object-oriented computer program in and of itself.

- Ruby, like Python and PERL, is a server-side programming language.

- Common gateway interface scripts can write in Ruby.

- Ruby is a programming language that may embed in HTML (HTML).

- Ruby has a simple syntax that a novice developer may pick up fast and effortlessly.

- Ruby's syntax is comparable to that of several other computer languages, including C++ and Perl.

- Ruby is incredibly scalable, and large projects created in Ruby are easy to maintain.

- Ruby may use to create web and intranet apps.

- Ruby can be installed on both Windows and POSIX systems.

- Many graphical user interface technologies, such as Tcl/Tk, GTK, and OpenGL, are supported by Ruby.

- Ruby can easily connect to DB2, MySQL, Oracle, and Sybase databases.

- Ruby includes many built-in functions that may use directly in Ruby scripts.

INTERESTING RUBY PROGRAMMING LANGUAGE FACTS

- Yukihiro Matsumoto created Ruby because he desired a scripting language that was more powerful than Perl and more object-oriented than Python.

- The name Ruby emerged from an online chat conversation between Matsumoto and Keiju Ishitsuka on February 24, 1993, before any program in the language had been created. Coral and Ruby were the first names offered. In an e-mail to Ishitsuka, Matsumoto chose the name Ruby.

- Ruby is sometimes mistaken for Ruby on Rails, a server-side framework written in Ruby under the MIT License that is used to develop web applications.

- Ruby's libraries and packages are handled via Rubygems, a centralized library management system.

- Ruby is unusual in the programming industry because it supports various programming paradigms, including procedural programming, object-oriented programming, and functional programming.

- The interactive Ruby interpreter (irb) may be used as a calculator.

- Ruby includes support for rational and complicated numbers, which aids with the solution of complex mathematical issues.

- Ruby supports code embedding. Ruby, for instance, may be integrated in Hypertext Markup Language (HTML).

- Dynamic typing and Duck typing are available to Ruby users.

- Ruby recognizes and uses "nil" instead of "null."

The following are the distinctions between Ruby and Ruby on Rails:

S. no.	Ruby	Ruby on Rails
01	Ruby, an object-oriented scripting language, debuted in 1995.	Ruby on Rails is an MVC-based web app development platform.
02	It's referred to as a general-purpose programming language.	It is renowned as a framework for data-driven web applications.
03	It was created in the computer language C	It was written in the Ruby programming language
04	It is regarded as a safe programming language.	While it is regarded to be more secure than Ruby.
05	It is not a structure.	Even though it is a web development framework.
06	Ruby is often used in the building of static websites.	When developing a static website, Ruby on Rails is typically not advised.
07	The Ruby programming language is said to be inspired by Perl and Smalltalk.	In that order, Ruby on Rails is said to be inspired by Django, Python's Laravel, and PHP.
08	Desktop apps are written in the Ruby programming language.	It is used to create web apps.
09	It was created using the user interface design approach.	It was created using the DRY and COC principles.
10	Its syntax is comparable to those of Perl and Python.	It has a syntax similar to Phoenix in Elixir and Python.
11	C++, Java, and VB.net are the most often utilized programming languages while creating apps.	HTML, CSS, JavaScript, and XML are the most often used languages when designing apps.
12	GitHub, Twitter, Airbnb, SCRIBD, Slideshare, Fiverr, and more significant firms use Ruby.	Bloomberg, Crunchbase, zendesk, PIXLR, and other leading firms use Ruby on Rails.

Index